Reel Power

OTHER BOOKS BY MARSHA SINETAR

Ordinary People as Monks and Mystics

Do What You Love, the Money Will Follow

Elegant Choices, Healing Choices

Living Happily Ever After

Developing a 21st-Century Mind

A Way Without Words

Self-esteem Is Just an Idea We Have About Ourselves

A Person Is Many Wonderful, Strange Things

Reel Power

Spiritual Growth Through Film

MARSHA SINETAR

TRIUMPH™ BOOKS
Liguori, Missouri

Published by Triumph™ Books
Liguori, Missouri
An Imprint of Liguori Publications

Library of Congress Cataloging-in-Publication Data

Sinetar, Marsha
    Reel power : spiritual growth through film / Marsha Sinetar. —
1st ed.
        p.   cm.
    Includes bibliographical references.
    ISBN 0-89243-529-1 : $9.95
    1. Spiritual life. 2. Motion pictures—Religious aspects.
    3. Motion pictures in religious education. 4. Self-actualization
(Psychology)—Religious aspects.   I. Title
    BV4501.2.S4727   1993
    261.5'7—dc20   92-44676
                                                                   CIP

First Edition

In memory of my good friend,
Gordon Johnson,
whose fine, wry humor I sorely miss.
I would have loved to discuss these films with you,
dear Gordon.

Contents

Acknowledgments

I began this book in early 1991, then spent two solid years altering and rewriting it. My neighbor, Gaynor Evitts, deserves high praise and thanks for her word processing help during these many months of manuscript revision. My longtime friend, Lyn DelliQuadri, came to my rescue with her editing expertise during the early stages of writing, and I heartily thank her. I'm enormously grateful to Patricia Kossmann of Triumph Books for her optimism about this work immediately upon reading the manuscript and I'm so thankful that she liked it. I also feel strangely indebted to all those bright actors and diversely gifted moviemakers whose virtue and light shine through their films. Like fine art, poetry and music, a good movie is lyrical and can open the eyes of our hearts.

Reel Power

Introduction

I picked a look you could understand.
—God (George Burns), *Oh, God*

Whoever we are, no matter what the unique call of our life, we are meant to learn a universal rule about personal fulfillment: Our own fundamental goodness brings us life, and brings it more abundantly. In other words, our innate virtue is our strength. Conversely, our base self is a killer. It always has been. In our heart, we know all this — such discoveries seem a central aim and realization of human existence.

If we're fortunate, we figure all this out on our own; the earlier the better. Sadly, most of us are experts at disowning our powers. We cast off our virtues, imagine that others — but not we — have the courage or compassion that we so crave. We identify with defeat, with hardship, with hopelessly shallow objectives or exploitive, anxious fellows. Deep down, however, almost everyone senses that there's more to life — if not in material attainments, then certainly in our most subjective, intimate experience. Despite life's varied convolutions, our most complete development as persons — what I've called *spiritual maturity* or optimal wholeness — happens when, and as, we express our decency. Of course this means we embrace our weaknesses and dark side too. But not as the dominant feature of our being.

All gestures of kindness and compassion, faithful commitment to integrity or excellence, our heroism, tenacity, or truthfulness, any relinquishment of narrow self-interest are only some of the many positive ways by which we assert our good will. These innumerable turnings — however small or subtle — reveal one inescapable fact: As we put our *best* self into our acts, deep healing and satisfaction results.

What Does "Heart" Mean?

To me the word *heart* means more than our primary physical organ, circulating blood through our body. It suggests, as Webster's dictionary puts it, "the seat of our vitality, intellect, emotion... the inner, central part of anything." Our heart contains the "hidden springs of our personal life... our entire mental and moral activity, both the rational and the emotional elements."[1] We conveniently forget this. Periodically, it helps to be reminded. Everything around us — books, poetry and art, nature, people — can aid our recollection.

The great theologian Martin Buber said it this way:

Existence will remain meaningless for you if you yourself do not penetrate into it with active love, and if you do not in this way discover its meaning for yourself. Everything is waiting to be hallowed by you.[2]

Apparently it is my life's call to talk of such sacred things. How then have I come to write a book about movies? Simply stated, motion pictures are spiritual guides to life. If we open the eyes of our hearts — that is, watch movies discerningly — films teach and reinforce lasting spiritual truths. That they don't always (or that we don't see or demand this) is quite beside the point. Just as great, grand lessons of personhood are contained in myths, in fables and fairy tales, so could it be with film. Movies are a significant, contemporary spiritual resource, a vehicle for communicating about our shared experience of being human.

With conscious selectivity, we can train our attention to penetrate into almost any story "with active love" and find lasting enrichment encoded in countless films. Most significantly, the best moving pictures reveal the best qualities of our own heart. Objectively observing ourselves while looking at films (I call this timeless practice *following breath*),[3] we will notice our flaws or shadows, *and* our vital, life-affirming impulses. *Any* infusion of greater inspiration or positivity to thought, feeling, or action, any movement at all of our will toward self-acceptance, kindness, patience, or charity indicates the presence of spirituality.[4] Finding in a film that which seeds true nourishment for our soul is better than gold.

With renewed inner sight, movies can transform our ordinary viewing, provide us with fodder for creative solutions, offer us new stories and inspiring models, and bring us into those elevated states of mind necessary for the growth we crave. These are all spiritual benefits. These revive us, bring us life.

In the words of William Blake (who was of course speaking about human perception, not cinema), movies benefit us when they help us "see things as they really are: Infinite." The brightest films — including animated stories — have always inspired and encouraged us.

The brightest, most spiritually aware individuals learn this by themselves. They have — as Chapter One suggests — *reel power:* the ability to dig out, and use, whatever is spiritually valuable in a movie. One such person is my friend and distant neighbor, Robert Thompson. Bob has loved and studied movies ever since he was a young boy. Now he owns and operates *Gualala Video,*[5] one of several local video stores. Bob's store is distinctive, incomparable; you can feel this the minute you enter. What's more, Bob is a perceptive diagnostician — he knows just what sort of movie you want to see. He started his video business when his private collection took over his home.

Finding the Mystical Message in Film

Of spirituality and film, Bob says, "Today, movies are a significant way most people can still get the mystical message." In his way, he explains what this means:

> For me, there's a magic in film — magic that people like Spielberg know about. And Capra. I've never felt this magic was totally under the control of the director, but rather that it came from a higher source. During my life, I've looked for the message (from the Creator?) through the medium of film.

Thompson points out that a film like *Zardoz* hints at the presence of a "mystical message" right from the start.

> The opening lines ask, "Is God in Show Business too?" Apparently so. Movies are a modern church — people look for their uplift from movies. Movies are also teachers. In *Bambi* we learn a large message: every time you get into trouble, The Father comes to your rescue. And *E.T.* also — when he points to his forehead and says, "I'll be home" — he's talking about spiritual reality — not about the sensory world.

If you think Bob is stretching a point, bear with me. Studying movies for their mystical message empowers us. We gain insight and greater self-awareness. We begin to appreciate our virtues and learn to "see" with our heart — understand the illogical aspects of human experience. We grow to comprehend love's odd, unwieldy nature — its many facets alive in us. This comprehension, soft though it may be, makes us smarter, helps us integrate intuition and logic. This is, in itself, a huge practical advantage, since most of life's problems stem from having too low a spiritual IQ — lack of whole thinking, the absence of what the Zen Buddhists call "a big mind, open mind," an inordinately polarized mentality.

So much of life today is centered on problems, recovery, and the painful struggles of *trying* to meet the unrelenting demands of twenty-first-century living. Unfortunately, by dwelling only on problems, and thus failing to see ourselves and our dilemmas in a heroic, promising light, we limit ourselves. Movies elevate our sights, enlarge imagination. Film, like poetry, is one of our heart's most subtle agents. It reminds us of what we know, helps us stretch and change, provides us with a sensory catalyst for creative, cutting-edge reflection.

This book states that *ordinary* movies can enrich us with answers for creative problem-solving. We can, and probably most of us unconsciously already do, use film to incubate fresh ideas to current dilemmas. For instance, a film's story and its characters show us how to reinvent (or "find") ourselves. Heroes and heroines (even when obviously stylized or faulty) are frequently models — blueprints for our minds. These patterns plant a sort of coded seedbed that somehow stimulate thinking beneath the level of awareness. In time, these codes sprout fruit of their own kind, ideas — for good or bad — for our life. As stated at the outset, as we identify ourselves with fundamentally good images, our soul gets nourished. This is no meager benefit: from our identifications flow the issues of our life.

It has been said that the soul has but two powerful faculties: its intellect and its will.[6] We can — if we watch movies intelligently — engage both our intellect and our will. Movies stimulate our best intentions and our desire to choose on behalf of whatever is intrinsically good, releasing the negative merely by noticing it.

We gain actual potency when combining this viewing method with our *application* of any lasting truths a movie gives us. We gain real power when we recognize (and *use*) the richness inherent in our whole mind, when we blend our rational and "irrational" processes. (Figuring out a film's symbolic or deeper meanings lets us practice this blending — just as poems, music, and literature serve us.) Hastily I add that this is art, not science.

All the movies in the world can't turn our beneficent desires into effective action. Only we have the power to act as we know we should — and can. But watching movies "with the eyes of our heart" certainly helps us identify our truest aims, finest values, and noblest aspirations.

Accepting Our Intrinsic Worth

A good deal is said these days about *denial*. Usually, this means a refusal to face one's problems or shortcomings. Here is, in part, how denial seems to work: A friend's young granddaughter (age six) had chicken pox. When her grandmother went to visit, she noticed that her grandchild had completely concealed her body by wearing a blue floor-length robe and long blue rubberized kitchen gloves (the kind used for washing dishes). She had also covered all her bedroom mirrors with newspapers. In answer to her grandmother's quizzical look, the little girl said, "I don't like seeing the spots on my hands or face."

Like that child, we deny our strengths and goodness (and our shortcomings). We routinely put on, as it were, protective coverings — in the form of unawareness, false humility, or debilitating physical symptoms — to mask our affections or aggressions, and certainly this represses our potential. Defending ourselves against the dangers of our own talents and truest perceptions is far less cumbersome than rising to the demands these place on us. The healthier we are, the more willing (and able) we are to risk removing our psyche's wraps.

Movies offer an unusually safe, enjoyable way to peek at all that we've denied — our dark sides and our light. Certainly films let us take a hard and frequent look at our unused powers, *if* we learn how to watch. No doubt, the decencies or courage we admire so much in lead characters are traits alive and well in us — although perhaps dormant or well-concealed.

Abraham Maslow's word on this is helpful: "it is precisely the god-like in ourselves that we are ambivalent about, fascinated by and fearful of, motivated to and defensive against. This is one aspect of the basic human predicament, that we are simultaneously worms and gods."[7] This book aims to introduce you to a way of watching films that connects you to your higher possibilities, shows you your best impulses and virtues while you're also being entertained. You may see that you've hidden your finest attributes by admiringly projecting these onto your favorite heroes and heroines. The rule of thumb on this is what we love in others is present in us (if also waiting to be developed).

Don't Dream It — Be It

I've said all this is art, not science. Like all art, the viewing method I'm suggesting will be interpreted and practiced slightly differently by each person. Like any art, the technique transforms us only if we perfect ourselves through diligent practice — when we *live* the art that's in us or penetrate our daily life with active love. In other words, we must try to use our "mystical messages" to restore our full engagement with life.

As we watch movies "with our heart," our mind receives its images in a solitary fashion, even if we're viewing while in the company of others. After a movie is over, if we've culled its deeper spiritual lessons, a time comes when we might want to apply these new understandings in daily life. This art asks our full focus, patience, and steady self-encouragement. It is one thing to mull over inspiring ideas in isolation, quite another to express these concretely in our everyday life or relationships. For this, we must admit we have potential, must refine our whole mind, *and* develop our good will.

It is, after all, through our mind that we raise or lower our sights about how to be human; but only through our positive acts of will can we bring our high visions to life. When we consciously improve our intellect and will, we can animate our lofty ideals into tangible, actual existence or clear out old, outmoded prejudices and crippling thought patterns. We don't become fully human by merely daydreaming about it. *The Rocky Horror Picture Show,* that cult favorite (but not one of mine), spells this out plainly: "Don't dream it, *be* it."

Being anything, and especially being whole or spiritually mature, calls for a partnership of mind and heart and will. As each chapter details, we can explore this linkage on our own, simply by raising our level of awareness as

we watch movies, through informal discussions, and by
further practice sessions of specific movies.

One of the best things about this method of movie
watching is that it's an engaging way to use leisure time
and relate to a film's story — much more fun than "zoning-
out," as my friends call their daydreamy, passive movie-
viewing. Perhaps zoning-out is a contemporary form of
managing stress.

Despite the continual pressures of contemporary life,
our minds are tremendously under-disciplined and under-
challenged. This is one reason most of us seek escape
through our common diversions or addictions. As that
mental giant Sherlock Holmes well knew, it's natural to crave chemical highs when one is not naturally
stimulated.

Holmes used cocaine when bored. Said he, in *A Scan-
dal in Bohemia*, "My mind rebels at stagnation — give me
problems, give me work... then I can dispense with artificial stimulation." Might this be true for us? I believe so.
Our life's most grand and selfless goals, exciting ones at
that, appear when we acknowledge our need for stimulation and responsibly step out to be all that we're born
to be.

Purposefulness is a primary characteristic of life. Each
of us yearns to discover *how* to use our existence meaningfully — how to do with life all that we know we were
meant to do. Whenever something blocks our creative, fulfilling expression, then (like Sherlock Holmes) we can feel
stagnant. Loss of joy and health may result. Naturally this
happens by degrees. The longer we're thwarted, or the
more talent we have, the greater our rebellion and sense
of despair.

In *Raging Bull*, Jake LaMotta (Robert De Niro) epit-
omizes the inevitable frustration, the erosion of virtue,
personal power, and hope when — for whatever reason —

someone's overarching destiny is hindered. If we weep uncontrollably while watching this film — as did a friend — we may have buried our talents, suppressed our own life. Tears, laughter, or rage are but messages from our heart that we can learn to interpret.

Our most worthy challenge is to reclaim our humanity, develop our fundamental goodness and high, fine, intelligible aims. This is a "mystical" ambition — inexplicable and enigmatic. It adds joy to the sweet mystery of our life. Growing toward our fullest expression of personhood is a private individual task and spiritual in the main. Each one names this activity in his or her own words and tackles it largely alone, in the safe, private corners of mind and heart — another reason why familiarizing ourselves with the motifs and patterns of our favorite films helps us grow.

Movies contain a mystical message whenever their stories strengthen our life's good purposes. They can remind us of our virtue, stimulate answers we're holding within ourselves, or show us what it means to be robustly and responsibly human. If we sense something fine in a film's movement and shadows, however subtle, if our imagination and inner person moves in closer to our decency and authentic life, our inner eyes (or mental vision) open. Then we comprehend the potentials and rich realities of our own splendid heart.

How To Use This Book

To make the best use of this book, I suggest three separate readings. The first could be handled as with any other book — read straight through to discover what's being said. The second time linger over the questions posed and compare your own insights with mine. The third reading could involve actually *doing* the journal (or discussion) exercises. These are provided to deepen self-awareness and cultivate a more vivid, mindful encounter with popular film.

Some readers who have never kept a journal may overcomplicate the process. They can relax. There's nothing to it — nothing more esoteric than making out a grocery list. Artists, scientists, musicians, craftpersons, and homemakers routinely write down their ideas or "to do" notes. They do so not because they're hopelessly self-absorbed but because they want to capture and save valuable information: their best thinking. Whether they scribble out recipes or formulas or middle-of-the-night revelations or quotes, whether they jot their notes down on napkin shreds or inside matchbook covers, their purpose is the same: to save some fleeting, but possibly precious, insight. Almost all creative people constantly attend to their mind's inner workings in some fashion. Even the Bible tells us to "Record the vision, and inscribe it on tablets" (Habakkuk 2:2).

Interpreting Your Viewing Habits and Choices

Every chapter in this book discusses movies — both old and new, both generally and specifically. No book, however, can say everything about a subject, and certainly nothing (no single book, lecture, or workshop) can itemize all the variables of an issue that might affect an individual. The mystical message in movies will become clearer to you as you look to movies (or television, plays, opera, books, etc.) to help you

- *imagine* new possibilities for yourself by acknowledging your existing — fundamental — strength, goodness, and resourcefulness.

- *contend* with your emotions, letting these serve — rather than thwart — your ideals, goals, growth, the adventure you want.

- *improve* your most intimate, inner conversations, images, and patterns of thinking, by becoming self-aware — especially of your subjective life.

Think about your own film preferences and viewing habits. Try to put this entire discussion into the context of your personal experiences and self-development. In Chapter Seven, I list some of my favorite films and suggest *specific* movies with journal (or discussion) questions to stimulate your inquiry. These motion pictures may not be relevant to you. You might prefer to interpret how you have, consciously or unconsciously, shaped your thinking, values, and growth through other films that you repeatedly watch. For instance, as a start, ask yourself:

- How have I used the often delicate, sometimes obvious, reality-forming images, sounds, and themes of movies to further my life's deepest needs and purposes?

- What specific heroes and heroines have lastingly impressed me? (What meaning do I give this?)

- What moods, qualities, attitudes, or values might I wish to gain (or create) from my viewing preferences?

- What inspires, moves, or challenges me in a film, particularly as this moves me away from fear toward more life, expanded awareness, or moral elevation?

- When do movies help me solve problems, incubate ideas, or find novel solutions?

As you work with this material and as you identify your favorite movies (the ones that empower you with hope, joy, or new, vital ideas), keep notes about the patterns of your discoveries: the types of movies you prefer, your consistent favorite characters or themes. Try to discern what these are — as metaphors — in terms of a message for your life.

Movies Have Their Limits

Not for a moment do I suggest that anyone substitute movie-viewing for therapy or for the nurture and support available within a competently run counseling group. On the other hand, therapists, counselors, liberal arts teachers, and parents who don't discuss popular films as they carry out their respective duties of healing, instruction, and the shaping of values sorely miss the mark of their true function. By helping those we mentor (and ourselves) *manage attention*, we further spiritual growth.

Movies have their limits. They are not prayer (except to those few saints for whom *everything* is prayer). Nevertheless, as later chapters show, by attending to our breath, by keeping a journal (as we watch a film), by taking stock of what we feel or think about some compelling bit of plot, dialogue, or character, we can befriend our hidden cerebrations and discover something new about ourselves. Certainly over time these practices help us guard our intellect, become discerning about what images, ideas, and words we invite into our heads through our eyes, ears, and attention. I can't understand why much more hasn't been made of the inherent value of movies long before now.

Those who don't like to write can form a discussion group on film's spiritual message with like-minded friends. Years ago, I joined a Great Books club. I'm not a joiner, and I skipped most meetings. Yet when I did attend it was richly rewarding. As a movie-lover, I've often wondered why so much of our socializing centers around excessive drinking, dining, and aimless chatter, and so little around movies. At any rate, if anything in this book enlivens good old-fashioned, heartfelt conversation, I for one will rejoice.

 1

...when you're born into this universe, you're in it for a long, long time.... After each lifetime there is an examining period... You see, every second of every lifetime is always recorded. And, as each one ends, we sort of look at it...examine it and then, if everyone agrees, you move forward — continue onward — [or you're sent back]. The point of this whole thing is to keep getting smarter, to keep growing, to use as much of your brain as possible.... Do you know [how much of your brain] you use?

—Bob Diamond
Defending Your Life

REEL POWER:
MINE "THE GOLD"
IN MOVIES

The work of art proceeds from the artist according to a model existing in the mind; which model the artist discovers...before he produces, and then he produces as he has predetermined.

—Saint Bonaventure

Everyone I know loves movies. The big screen, the dark theater, the shared experience with all those anonymous heads, even the smell of popcorn are irresistible forces. I used to think that these drew us into a fragile rainbow of fantasy, let us live an enhanced reality at thirty-six frames per second. Or is it twenty-four? Whatever. Once technology was capable of mass-producing movies on videotape for our solitary delectation in front of small, private TV screens, it took only a split second for millions of us movie lovers to buy or rent not just our favorite classics but whatever was left on the shelves. Forget big screens, shared experiences, and the fact that, at home, we pop our own popcorn. Now it's clear to me: The movie itself has power. And what real power this is.

Even an ordinary movie is potentially liberating; it need *not* be extraordinary in its technical, artistic, or conceptual presentation to exert influence. Our conscious mind, programmed as it is by culture and the context of existence, fixes solely on what's visible. Normally, we attach ourselves to places, to creative projects or things. Attachments stupefy — render us helpless. Perhaps we're wrapped up tightly in our most limiting beliefs, muddled about our potential, or still at the effect of childish feelings and dependencies. To widen our scope, movies need only tell us stories that we see as ours, that give us glimpses — however fanciful — of our obsessions or difficulties, or they need only bring us hope.

Stories enlarge us, help resolve fears, restore us as particular, distinctive individuals with as yet unrealized dreams. Stories can activate our inner power to choose goodness, vitality, and love. Saint Paul described these higher experiential realms. He prayed (and I paraphrase here) that the eyes of our heart might become enlightened that we may know what is the hope of God's calling for us.[1]

Most people, however, seem to prefer safety. They shun the exhilarating heights of their own advanced awareness. Watching films alertly gives us a way to inch toward the truth. In relative comfort we spot self-deception, remembering who we are at our best.

Movies are often parables that retell myths. As Jung wrote, myths are not precisely fiction but rather deep, abiding truths about reality that humankind needs to have affirmed again and again. In these pages I suggest that movies are psychically productive even when they're obvious, elementary fairy tales. A very simple story reinforces life's tough truths and therefore teaches us to endure or to apply ourselves fruitfully.

Of course, *all* truly fine art encourages self-examination and honesty. Ancient sages and contemporary psychologists alike insist that music, art, and drama are potent transformers of consciousness. The medium of film blends all facets of art in a uniquely riveting way. Like consciousness itself, film engages our senses, intellect, and heart, capturing our attention so completely that we can enter the world of self-perception.

Opportunities like this are hard to come by in the distracted, anxious rush of daily living. As we become self-aware viewers, our psyche's hidden content — our heart — reveals itself, peeps out at us hesitatingly, in dreams, in sudden insights, through the "Aha!" experience. This book's viewing method invites you to consider your favorite movies as spiritual guides to life — not merely as sources of escapist entertainment.

Projections of Our Heart

Christ's admonition that we stop worrying about the splinter in our brother's eye and, instead, remove the log from our own, gives timeless weight and testimony to the phenomenon of projection. We imagine that others, but not we, are ridden with vice. We disassociate ourselves from our deceits and cowardice but easily fantasize that family or coworkers have magical powers to manipulate us or dangerously control our fate. We disown our life's vitality by this displacement — not simply by failing to acknowledge our negative, self-sabotaging habits but also by never learning to transmute these qualities into viable, life-sustaining powers. We magnify the capabilities of friends and strangers, positive and negative, then feel ineffectual and wanting in their midst. Thus we escape the consequences of our potential and miss the mark of responsible, truthful engagement with our own experience.

Film (indeed all art) lets us see ourselves anew. Movies

can show us where we store our "logs." Through our intense, sometimes inexplicable feelings or reactions to a character or plot, we can recover our own powers — for both good and evil.

Our interpretation of stories is influenced by our personal history, particularly our pattern of psychological disownments. All rejected, unacceptable bits of self are, in fact, untapped powers, unassimilated and thwarted talents, vibrancies awaiting productive release. These castoffs are forceful enough to impair awareness, and isolate us in a fictitious, self-invented world. Instead of accepting and expressing our feelings and ideas, we project them onto others, "visualize in the outside world those parts of [our] own personality with which [we] refuse to identify ourselves."[2]

If we look at films to seek out their mystical messages, we become aware of our projections and those of the storytellers. A movie's characters then convey a two-pronged message: the superficial issues of the plot line and the deeper ones of the character's projection.

As we yearn — breath and hands held tight — for the hero to save the helpless, cowering victim, we're really rooting for our own rejected heroism, our incapacities or powerlessness. When we cheer some character's wit or ingenuity, we do so with and only because of our good store of humor and resourcefulness.

We may most easily resist our fundamental good. It is usual for us to embrace our dark side (despite the exhortations to the contrary by theologians, social "scientists," and educators). Guilt, shame, helplessness — these we know too well. Our inherent integrity is something else again — much more difficult for us to swallow. I reinforce this point throughout this book to help us light up our hidden virtue. I believe virtue is synonymous with *authentic* human power.

Authentic power is what we humans love and hate, simultaneously crave and fear. We take two steps toward vigorous, truthful engagement with life and then take three steps back. Yet it is through our virtues that we grow responsibly, safely, and purposefully. I repeat: We project our fundamental human decency, yet decency is what, collectively and individually, we must reclaim — and soon.

The challenge of human growth in modern culture offers precisely what it always has: the chance and obligation to explore our deepest heart, and the subsequent necessity to discover fresh, broad means by which to lighten-up, expand, elevate our consciousness, cant it toward its highest realms. Our mind's shift toward the new idea or the symbolic and concrete affirmation of life releases energy, invites healthy rebirth. If not at once, then gradually.

As we experience the radical changes of the twenty-first century, movies seem a primary way for us to find provocatively useful "stuff": images, metaphors, and psychic notions to help us imagine big, creative solutions or what it might take to live our own largest humanity. If we can see the log in our own eyes *and* our heroism, compassion, and power, we can do ourselves and one another a world of good.

Creative, inspired thinkers have always recognized this tie between art, spirituality, and everyday experience. As I do in these pages, a special few even discuss the spiritual potential in movies per se. India's Meher Baba (thought by many to be an Avatar — Perfect Master, a God-realized being) considered film a significant carrier of spiritual truth. He refused to concede "fictitious cleavages in the unity of life," and never exaggerated the differences between the products of daily life and the Indivisible Truth living behind all created things. This perception is a key to the power I'm describing.

Despite the fact that Meher Baba spent most of his life

in India, in total silence and relative seclusion, he reminded filmmakers — as well we should today — that they had an important responsibility to humankind:

> The film should ask itself whether it is utilizing its spiritual potential to the full so that man may be helped in his search for Truth, or is merely pandering to his pleasure in the false; whether it is encouraging, or retarding youth's inner growth with an overdose of sex and crime films; and whether it is striving after wealth and fame at the cost of man's inherent thirst for the spiritual and the uplifting.[3]

Meher Baba saw the obvious: that film is a uniquely potent medium. Exploring the leverage for intelligent self-transformation that movies provide, we gain tremendous strength, interior sureness. This leverage is pay dirt to the development of our higher attributes: intuition, whole — nondual — thinking, the productive use of all our varied intelligences. We glean *ourselves* from the best images and forms ingested. What we see in those characters we most admire, we appreciate from the exact qualities within. Yet movies are often overlooked or denigrated, considered "passive" entertainment — part of popular, as opposed to erudite, culture.

I contend that film's mass appeal is one of its most positive characteristics, making it an ideal vehicle for furthering personal growth. After all, look what happened to culture and universal literacy after the printing press made books widely available. Myths, fables, fairy tales, the parables of scripture are not elitist teachers. Rather these are populist tools, timelessly encouraging human dignity and growth. The same is true of movies. For those intellectuals who hold pop-culture in contempt, for all those whose ennui is too well-developed, psychiatrist Dr. Thomas Szasz's comment applies: "Boredom is the feeling that everything is a waste of time; serenity is that nothing is." While certain films are obviously richer, more positive, and creatively intelligent than others, when we mine a movie for its gold, far from wasting our time, its story may enrich us immeasurably.

Properly watched, motion pictures give us more than merely a few hours carefree respite from our day-to-day involvements. Films can be consciousness-raising tools; their stories are personal mentors that lessen fear or illuminate the love, virtue, and wholeness already present in our lives.

For these purposes, the best films, however crude or otherwise elementary their themes, also reinforce the reality principle. From the reality principle we learn to grapple with life — not avoid it. "Everything is waiting to be hallowed" by us. This is one mystical message, pure gold, hidden in all valuable stories.

To See or Not To See

People frequently ask how to approach films overloaded with gratuitous sex, violence, or negativity (however they define these terms individually). One friend wondered,

Suppose I'm out for the evening with ten pals all wanting to see *The Texas Chainsaw Massacre* or even a fine film like *Bugsy.* I'm forced to go along. How best to watch these?

Moving pictures are encoded plays of consciousness, codes and patterns about reality. While it is not my intent to censor anyone or proselytize, the method in this book can help us discern the value of whatever reality-codes we're ingesting.

Movies seem to me like books or people. We're rarely "forced" to spend time with them against our will. We read our favorite books with different purposes in mind (e.g., for diversion, comedic — or horrific — relief, etc.) and can see any movie for varied reasons as well, sociability being one.

With my method, we can watch movies while keeping an eye on their overall humanity or philosophy of life. We know what it's like to put down a boring book or one with overly explicit, to us distasteful, violent or sexual text. Putting a book down is, frankly, our existential adult choice. Common experience also tells us what it's like to visit with a friend or family member who's severely depressed, or mentally ill, and whose absorption with the dark, underbelly of life is excessive — perhaps, to us, unwholesome. As individuals, *we* elect how involved and enmeshed we'll get with their thinking.

Similarly, we must take notice if we regularly enjoy imprinting the images of depressed, depressing movies on our minds. It is beyond the scope of either this book or my intentions to spell out a finite, moral blueprint for your movie viewing. Not *every* movie is useful to further spiritual growth; not every movie need be seen. Who watches what is an issue bound up with world-view, one's overall life posture.

In *Crimes and Misdemeanors*, one of Woody Allen's characters reflects on just this theme. Two brothers, a rabbi and a doctor, are arguing about how best to handle a family crisis. The rabbi reduces their battle to their differing world-view, saying something like,

We've been having this argument since we were kids. It boils down to the fact that you see no hope or moral order in the world, and I believe that the universe is full of moral order, love, and forgiveness.

I personally immerse myself in movies whose filmmakers honestly believe (and support my belief) in a universe laced through and through with hope, moral order, love, and forgiveness. You can use this book's method to observe your own world-view, to determine what you will — or won't — welcome into your mind's storehouse of images.

Movies tell us what to think about ourselves. A collaborative art form, films represent the ideas and artistry of multiple psyches. We must select movies wisely — in order not to be cast down by the imaginations of a creative team who may not be artists of the highest caliber or intention. This seems a matter for individual discernment.

When the psychic projections of moviemakers uplift us, we are renewed, and we turn toward life in fresh, surprising ways. Whether we realize it or not, art presents us with a way to organize experience, especially as it relates to inner growth and problem-solving. An architect I know examines a movie's sets whenever she starts a new building project. A socialite studies its costumes. A recently divorced man selects films about starting over in mid-life. There is no end to the novel information we get from film. Movies ask us deep questions — ones we may avoid *or* continually ask ourselves; they give us a chance to forget our problems while, unconsciously, we keep working on them.

Given film's transforming powers, it seems time to consider the mind of those who make our movies. What do filmmakers hope to teach us? What are their values, visions, or inner strivings and disturbances? Do they merely crave our money? Frank Capra is not alone in wanting more. He gives us vivid, clear examples of ourselves at our best — even as we are "only human." Of his own vision, Capra once said:

My films will explore the heart not with logic, but with compassion...I will deal with the little man's doubts, his causes, his loss of faith in himself, in his neighbor, in his God. And I will show the overcoming of doubts, the courageous renewal of faith...And I will remind the little man that his mission on earth is to advance spiritually....[4]

Capra's vision was large-minded. Even lesser intellects and films contribute mightily to our varied hearts, our doubts, overcomings, and spiritual ascensions.

Reel Power:
Active, Conscious, Transformational Viewing

Singly and collectively we have undervalued cinema as one of our era's liveliest storytellers about our own humanity. Unfortunately, we've inflated film's importance in other realms — like trend or opinion-setting or its various escapist options. People often attend movies to withdraw from reality, not to find clues about Ultimate Reality. Motion pictures have become, for some, a kind of junk food — empty, even toxic to life's healthiest impulses. When, for instance, we mindlessly watch films or television, our hypnotic state absorbs the banal and superficial. These images corrode our imagination, draw us progressively downward into a herd mentality, or distance us from our actualizing self. To nourish daily life, the deeper things of spirit often require active concentration, steady chewing-up, and thorough assimilation.

Newspapers frequently report that teenagers are occasionally so overstimulated by a film's violence that they break out in fights directly after (or even during) the show. We hear of adults who believe that in order to live the good life they must be as rich or physically attractive as their favorite stars. They've never defined "the good life" for themselves, coveting instead those affectations that promise fulfillment by means of a sculpted physique, a Rolls Royce, or a customized kitchen. Comparing themselves to a Madonna or Stallone they feel inadequate. The popular, oft-repeated motto, "A woman can never be too thin or too rich," bears this out. People cannot digest the idea that inner joy has little to do with good looks or wealth when they feed steadily on false ideas — those that divert attention from what is decent and fine within.

To find the mystical message in film we must have an active, discriminating focus. Related to the "to see or not to see" question, movies seem most helpful (i.e., for our productive, wholesome growth) when they raise awareness about what it means to be authentically ourselves and fully human.

Put in this frame, it's easy enough to see why a tediously grizzly *Texas Chainsaw Massacre* or the truly pointless *Friday the Thirteenth* series have "no raison d'être" (to quote Halliwell's summation on the latter), but why a *Godfather* or *Citizen Kane* or *Bugsy* (with their depth and complex portrayals of human vice and torment) shed light on the demonic side of our experience. Again, not *every* movie intends to be a spiritual masterpiece. Some start out as mental junk. So what?

Not every shred of food we eat is good for us, but still we consciously crave our share of grease and sweets now and then, and come away dizzy with delight — just for the fun of it, for the sociability, the diversion. If we lack discernment, if fat and sugar are all we seek (and all we eat), ah well, then that's another matter. Nature deals justly with us: as we sow, so shall we reap. If we identify with the worst in life, that's exactly what we get. So too with mental food — the more nutritious our fare, the better.

If we find in a story's content or in its symbolic cues and energies information about that which is sublime or struggling in us (because we are alive, have "is-ness" — sheer being) then instead of being exploited by films, we'll align ourselves with the richest messages emanating from a screenwriter's consciousness.

We can look to characters, to dialogue, and to the story's *animating essence* (its spirit, its attributes of virtue or humanity) to discover our latent courage or worth. Instead of unconsciously swallowing idealized images of popularly valued items or fragments of appearance, matters of taste, we can "single out the best" human conduct and redeeming characteristics that we can find.[5] The most noble acts and high, redeeming values in a movie align us with whatever creative intelligence exists in us. This pairing or alignment of spiritual projections — ours and the moviemakers' — moves us forward, however slightly, into restored relationship with our own animating essence.

Stimulating Love, Virtue, and Breath

Watching films in this fashion, it helps to think of ourselves as detectives, searching for The Good (defined by Kierkegaard as one thing in its essence, and — like love — the same thing in each of its diverse expressions). We preserve and build our power as sentient, responsible, and creatively intelligent persons when we

- *follow the love (agape) in a movie:* we find, study, and reflect on what are called Being values such as joy, courage, truth, honesty, faithfulness, playfulness, productivity, and creativity;

- *follow its virtues:* we identify and notice whatever fundamental purity or life-affirming power exists in a story — and in us;

- *follow our own breath:* we stay alert to our physical and emotional reactions to the story (and all its variables, like characters, imagery, or dialogue) so as to understand what inspires or depletes us.

Later chapters develop each of these three points. For now suffice it to say that movies mirror us and invite us to go beyond the obvious. Their themes and images can powerfully equip us to see ourselves as we are at our worst, and at our best, or help us invent new scripts about who we hope to be. Our power — and lasting enjoyment — comes from finding the enduring value of truths in a movie and using our discoveries to further our growth as persons. Like classic fables and especially the simpler fairy tales, this modern-day electronic art need only be sincere to touch us. Moreover, each story moves each person slightly differently.

As individuals, we have unique psychological and spiritual battles to wage if we would experience spiritual health and wholeness. There is gold in almost all stories, if we stay alert enough to the prospecting process to dig it out. "Gold" means whatever profits us, usually that which is of our spiritual self. This is the hidden, mystical message. As one ancient text put it, gold is "light, life, immortality ... to 'refine' this 'gold' is to burn away from our spiritual Self the dross of all that is not Self. Hence it is a 'golden' cord by which [we] human puppets are rightly guided."[6]

If we link some secret, holy remnant of ourselves to some shine in a story, we can better accept and activate that shred of self toward healthier expression. Our identifications and projections help us locate our productive or generous traits and, eventually, we may consciously opt to exercise these. When our connections with a story have been honest, after a film is over, what was previously our unconscious projection frequently rises to conscious awareness. Our angers or annoyances, our dreams or conversations, may spotlight what we need to do or want to be to polish up a small corner of ourselves. Here is where prudent, resourceful interplay of intellect and will becomes critical. Perhaps at first we simply focus our attention on one trait or a single unexpressed need.

Our focus of attention is light. As Haverstock (Joel McCrea) warns in *Foreign Correspondent*, "Hang on to your lights, they're the only lights left in the world!" In time, we improve an attitude or behavior in the area under examination. This is precisely how self-respect and wholeness are enhanced: by *living* all the traits, values, and actions we know have worth.

Those who crave optimal psychological health are *self-creators*. They are hunters, unearthing language, symbols, and meaningful contexts by which to discover, rediscover, and reveal the darkness and the sweetness of their own souls. They express themselves creatively by giving *authentic outer shape* to whatever they sense to be valid within this, while sustaining the reality that they are imperfect and flawed. Stories in film (precisely like those in books and the preliterate, oral tradition of folktales) illuminate our shadowy, unrealized world. These give us ways and means to understand what we are avoiding, what we need or want to be and do next.

Effectively Using the Mind's Riches

The truly intelligent are full of common goodness and practical resourcefulness. As a matter of course, their minds transcend problems, playfully enjoy the problem-solving process. Such people engage fully with life, they fear less and love more. By "truly intelligent" I don't mean simply having a high IQ (as traditionally measured by standard tests) but rather having cultivated and *integrated* all one's intelligences: logic and intuition, for instance, rational and "irrational" faculties like dreams or hunches.[7] With our whole mind, we resolve paradoxes, or figure a way out of trouble when, at first, we were sure there was no way out. All these advantages, and more, are but facets of normal, creative intelligence. We love 007, Sherlock Holmes, The Thin Man, and Agatha Christie's Miss Marple and Hercule Poirot because, in part, they model our creative, resourceful brightness.

The greater our awareness of the riches of our *own* mental capacities, the more effortlessly and spontaneously we serve our own and others' interests. Otherwise, we're miserably entrenched, stupid really — stuck decade after decade in fear or some hopeless dilemma, unable to extricate ourselves. Unintelligence — the lopsided, fragmented use of our mind — results in fear, anger, victimization, abuse, the denial of hypocrisies. This seems the primary plague of humankind.

In *Defending Your Life*, Daniel (Albert Brooks) is a borderline case. He's on hold between life and death while his days on earth are being scrutinized for signs of intelligent life. His examiners represent the universe, which wants Daniel to have developed his mind's powers enough to move on and contribute to the next phase of cosmic life. Bob Diamond (Rip Torn) is Daniel's defender. He explains how inordinate fear prohibits evolutionary growth and cripples the mind:

> ...being from earth as you are, and using as little of your brain as you do, your life has pretty much been devoted to dealing with fear. Everyone on earth deals with fear. That's what *little brains* do.

...fear is like a giant fog. It sits on your brain and blocks everything: real feelings, true happiness, real joy. They can't get through that fog. But you lift it and, Buddy, you're in for the ride of your life.

I propose that the "ride of our life" is essentially spiritual — dependent on the effective use of our mind's highest attributes: whole perception, creativity, intuition, honesty and compassion, courage, good humor.[8] All these unseen, spiritual faculties flow, synergistically, from our mental realms. These alone transmute fear into love, and help us turn the negative aspects of life into more positive experiences and outcomes. The stories and characters of films (and naturally some more than others) inform our intellect about its own divine, creative nature. This must be why scripture warns us to "cast down every vain imagination" — anything that would take us away from our own good.

The movies mentioned in this book demonstrate that it is desirable and entirely reasonable to expect to find information about wholesome values and qualities in popular entertainment. To achieve this, we need storytellers and filmmakers with deep spiritual insight and elevated levels of awareness. Stories like *Dances with Wolves, Awakenings,* and *Gandhi* illustrate such filmmakers exist and that box-office success and inspiring stories are not alien to each other.

Nevertheless, a movie that touches us profoundly may not appeal to critics. Something little — a tender mannerism, a bright color, a character's change of mind, some softening of anger or enchantment of choice — so easily speaks to our hearts because, ultimately, our hearts are rich with untapped virtue.

In *Do the Right Thing* Spike Lee repeated a motif — three good friends, dressed in white, seated casually in front of a vibrant, poppy-colored wall. They're chewing the fat. Lee's choice of vivid earth tones, his cinematic kindness toward the ordinary — the sweet familiarity of old pals sharing time — sparked warmth and nostalgia in me, summoning fond memories of places and friends, time spent talking of nothing and feeling at home in the world. The upshot of these uneventful times is indeed profound. Lee touches nerves of love, revives affections long forgotten. This is spiritual — a gift from his heart to ours. No small matter, in the spiritual scheme of things.

"Watch over your heart with all diligence," cautions Proverbs 4:23, "for from it flow the springs of life." Our very life takes shape from seemingly inconsequential offerings.

When I saw *Emma's Shadow*[9] (a fairy tale for people of all ages, about a little girl's rite of passage into compassionate love), one silent, visual moment at the end of the film — Emma's reunion with her friend Malthé — stirred deep, painful compassion in me. Emma puts her small child's forehead on Malthé's adult brow and leans on him as if for life itself. To me, her gesture communicated the highest order of what is termed *agape* (benevolent, self-sacrificing, vulnerable, compassionate love). Emma's posture — her helpless giving-up of self in love — suggests that this love continually surrounds us. *Agape* fuels our life. This love is gold. It's found right in front of us, where we don't often think to look.

A movie's visual nuances may remind us of our existing virtues or show us that some essential fragment of ourselves awaits rebirth through our identifications, choices, and commitments. The greater our ability to *use* film (instead of being used *by it*), the more likely it is our identification will provide further unseen steps by which we edge toward the robust inner health we want.

2

*[My grandpa] says most people nowadays are run by fear:
fear of what they eat, fear of what they drink, fear of their
jobs, their futures, fear of their health. They're scared to
save money and scared to spend it....*

*[His pet aversion] is the people who commercialize on fear,
you know — they scare you to death so that they can sell
you something you don't need — So he sort of taught us to
do what we want to do, and not be afraid of anything....*

—Alice
You Can't Take It with You

ADOPT NEW STORIES
AND STATES OF MIND

When [a movie is good it is] the result of some inner belief which is so strong that you show what you want in spite of a stupid story.[1]

— Jean Renoir

As Director Jean Renoir tells us, pictures are about a *state of mind*. Our task, as spiritually inclined viewers, is to locate, then study, movies that advance us as whole persons, or — as discussed, conversely — notice if we prefer perverseness (and thereby cultivate despairing, negative attitudes). All good stories, in almost any film, can improve self-understanding or show us the next steps we need to take to reach new levels of development, spotlighting the potential of our hidden strengths and values.

In *Chariots of Fire*, Eric Liddell, a Scottish missionary, uses his running prowess to glorify God. During the trials of the 1924 Olympics, Liddell realizes that the 100-meter heat, in which he is scheduled to compete, falls on a Sunday — his Sabbath or day of rest. Liddell consciously chooses to drop out of the race. A stunned British Olympic Committee (which includes the Crown Prince of England) gathers itself in an immense, ornate ballroom to persuade

Eric to change his mind. The Committee cannot believe that their strongest and favorite runner would pull out of the race for so trivial a reason as his faith. But the young missionary's mind is made up:

> I'm afraid there are [no two ways out of this]...I cannot run on the Sabbath and that's final....God made countries and God makes kings and the rules by which they govern....Those rules say the Sabbath is His and I for one intend to keep it that way.[2]

Just in time another athlete interrupts and resolves the stalemate by saying he'll switch places with Eric. As the Committee leaves the meeting room, the Duke of Sutherland gives thanks that Eric stuck to his guns:

> The "lad"...is a true man of principle and a true athlete. His speed is a mere extension of his life, its force. We sought to sever his running from himself.[3]

Watching *Chariots of Fire* we too intuitively know that Liddell's values, virtues, and his vocation (who he is as a particular person; how he *lives* his uniqueness) are tightly interwoven strands of his power. Liddell's conscious choice not to run against his values adds weight and credibility to his vitality as a human being. This "vitality of self" — the affirmative drive within our healthiest impulses — is a key to opening our inner eyes and thereby moving incrementally toward wholeness.

Nuts serves as another example of the way a popular, quite ordinary, film might encourage growth. *Nuts* tells the story of a bright, powerful, and confused woman caught in a tangle of unproductive choices. The heroine, Claudia Draper (Barbra Streisand), is a call girl. She's accused of murder and struggling to stay sane amidst contaminated, mixed messages from people who *say* they love her but who continually undermine her humanity and welfare. Claudia's painful childhood — sexual abuse by one parent, alternating possessive, toxic "love" and willful neglect by the other — disrupts her stability. Claudia has never learned to communicate so that others *hear* her. This isolation, in part, keeps her half-crazed.

Intelligent, chic, and by all outward appearances successful, Claudia is nevertheless a fake — a fugitive from life. Her role as a prostitute seems a handy metaphor for her life's ills. She shuts her eyes to her pain, to the illusory world of illicit sex, counterfeit power, and superficial affluence. Not surprisingly Claudia is enraged. Film critic Roger Ebert described her as, "so filled with anger that the specific targets hardly matter; the whole world is her target."[4]

Perhaps we identify with Claudia's frustration. Only the spiritually immature expect inner peace without first engaging with, and reconciling, old simmering conflicts. Until Claudia deals truthfully with her gut-wrenching early abuses — until she effectively communicates her suppressed rage to her betrayers — adult joy, love, and a meaningful life will elude her. So it is with us. The movie could help those with unfinished childhood business come to terms with their own next steps.

Nuts is a slick courtroom drama with somewhat cardboard characters and a predictable plot. Most of us would not call it a "fine film." Nevertheless *Nuts* can be a decent, constructive story for those adults in recovery, whose personal history matches Claudia's. *Nuts* underscores the obvious: inner development precedes all satisfactory resolution of outer conflict. Claudia's solutions may well pinpoint our own *un*intelligence, our life's glaring psychological assignments. To gain fulfillment as adults we too must cultivate skillful means — appropriate actions — by which to acknowledge, then cast out, personal demons. This movie's merit is its fairy tale instruction: true inner peace is costly, is no cheap grace.

Like all helpful tales, *Nuts* reinforces the idea that struggle is an integral part of every life, a key to enduring happiness, and that we do well not to avoid it. *Nuts* is a fairy tale for grown-ups. The movie emphasizes what Freud and, later, child psychologist Bruno Bettelheim (among others), referred to as *the reality principle:* Fairy tales teach youngsters to live in reality. They illuminate — sometimes viciously — the dangers of unreality. Odd as it seems, this basic lesson of childhood is simultaneously an elementary spiritual principle, a primal comprehension of our heart. Any movie, "fine film" or crass, that underscores this precept helps us grow more fully human — if we know how to see.

Using Film as Fairy Tales

Bruno Bettelheim's research on the value of fairy tales immeasurably increased my interest in both fairy tales and in film as resources for healthy adult growth. Bettelheim suggests that the best stories (i.e., those proving most productive to our long-range welfare) teach children that outer success alone cannot quiet their *inner* anxieties. Children, and adults too, hunger for information about what, other than sheer physical power (which most people lack) or power over others (which almost no one has) is needed to triumph in life:

> Fairy tales suggest that it is less impressive deeds which count ... an inner development must take place for the hero to gain true autonomy. Independence and transcending childhood requires personality develop-

ment, not becoming better at a particular task or doing battle with external difficulties.[5]

In this era of unbridled anxiety over economic, social, and personal uncertainty, adults can use film to gain their bearings just as children use fairy tales: as tools to build higher, more complex levels of development; as catalysts, organizers, or soothers of their mind's irrational processes; and as teachers instructing them to face life's harsh truths.

Who among us viewing *Bugsy, Power, Wall Street,* or *Reversal of Fortune* (all diverse commentaries about wealthy, yet emotionally twisted, adults) doesn't grasp the fact that affluence, leisure time, physical attractiveness, and even superior intelligence are, by themselves, insufficient factors for harnessing either substantive gratification, creativity, or lasting joy? Fairy tales — and film as fairy tale — stress that hard work, perseverance, and human virtue are requisites for lasting personal fulfillment.

Simple, instructive stories (like *Dances with Wolves* or Christy Brown's autobiography, *My Left Foot*) are spiritually uplifting fairy tales (if not something larger, like myth) when they portray our dark sides and inadequacies and show us how to live with or transcend these. Seeing the film based on Christy Brown's life story or the more recent *Awakenings,* we feel, and somehow learn, that every human spirit is freed by its own *inner* depths: healthy, hopeful attitudes, compelling vision, perseverance, good will, a love of life, or the striving to transmute misfortune into personal triumph. Such movies invite us to rejoin our own dynamic interiority and show another vital attribute — inner power — that each of us possesses.

Recently when addressing a college audience, I read a short excerpt from *My Left Foot* to emphasize that optimism is an inherent factor in true spirituality. The passage, in Brown's own words, described his joyful liberation upon

finally learning to write — and type — with his left foot. After my lecture, an audience member told me that his young,
severely arthritic son had been tremendously inspired by
viewing, and re-viewing, the movie. Said the father, "The
movie was good therapy for him. During his darkest hours
it gave him hope and courage." Directly following him was
a woman who confided that simply *hearing* the reading of
Brown's remarks shocked her into realizing that she could
face (indeed, she *wanted* to face) her own obstacles: lack of
formal schooling and a strong belief that she was "too old"
to try anything new. Such desire is spiritual — our impulse
to live as fully as we were meant to. Both the woman and
the young arthritic boy were learning the reality principle
from a movie.

Through Fantasy We Study Reality

Although there is no clear-cut line separating myth, fable, and fairy tales, the fairy tale tends to be gentler, more
optimistic, and fairly obvious in stating that our higher humanity requires us to meet reality as it is and as we are,
right now.[6] Even the silliest films can open our eyes in this
fashion and reinforce our good intentions. For example,
Home Alone is a comedy about a boy whose parents ab-
sentmindedly leave him home — alone — when they rush
off to their Paris vacation. The 8-year-old finds he must
protect his family home from two dim-witted burglars. He
confronts his fear in an uncomplicated, hilarious way, after accepting the do-or-die nature of his circumstance. His
comprehension hits him all at once. We see this mere twig
of a boy rush down the hall into the bathroom to cope with
his abandonment.

His first (apparently favorite and much repeated) solution is to spray his father's deodorant under his innocent,

hairless little armpits. He seems to get a squirt of courage each time he borrows this symbol of masculinity from his father's adult reality. He eventually outwits his adversaries with various tricks and ploys, all artfully constructed to obstruct the two moronic robbers.

The fact that all these antics are *unreal* actually aids our absorption of universal truths about reality. A story's improbability often ensures receptivity to its deeper ideas. Through artful fantasies, we allow practical messages into our awareness. Too-realistic portrayals rob us of much needed filtering and inner "play."

When a group of children were surveyed about why they liked *Home Alone*, they said the story reminded them of times when they were left alone to fend for themselves. They seemed to get a literal message that "...it's possible to defend your house if someone breaks in."[7] Adults enjoy the film when their minds sense deeper universal truths in it. As in *Nuts*, *Home Alone* repeats the reality principle: the key to true success is a character's *inner* development (e.g., wit, boldness, fortitude, etc.) and his or her ability to face life's challenges. Surely if we look around us — at people we admire in our families or communities — we observe this rule in action.

More than any outer accomplishment in *Home Alone* (the house, as it turns out, is completely trashed by the boy's solutions), the little hero's subjective enhancements are what we visualize or borrow for ourselves much as children play with or use their parents' possessions — like deodorant — to reinforce their growth or their will to survive.

We adults carry small children around in us, as us. If we would be authentic, autonomous, and fully functioning, we must develop these younger energies or awarenesses. Generally this means facing our fears and standing up to life's challenges. Movies are a readily available helpmate in this ongoing process of becoming. This is particularly true when we know ourselves to be, in the main, effective persons, headed toward the upper reaches of a productive, creative life. Then we pursue wholesome adventure and want stories that further our advancement as capable persons.

Most adults experience what some pop-psychologists now call our "inner child." As we restore our highest spiritual faculties, bring to life our vital interior processes, our creative gifts, and our unseen impulses for love and life, our mind hungers for the stimulation of fantasy. One reason that scriptures like the Holy Bible, the Bhagavad-Gita, and other sacred writings are enduring life companions is that these convey truth through vivid stories, earthy parables, and dramatic conflicts.

New Stories for New Powers

As a child, I loved to play with the workings of my mind. Early on, I discovered that thoughts were *things*, if unseen. They shifted about and could be directed. Thoughts seemed to me a malleable substance — the plastic, permeable links by which to construct daily life itself. My mind could substitute one idea for another (just like exchanging colorful baseball cards with my friends, but invisibly). I regularly traded in fearsome pictures for bright, engaging ones. Thoughts replaced direct experience and then somehow produced it. (Later in life, the adage "Whatever you focus on grows stronger in your life" partially explained this phenomenon.)

I didn't realize until adulthood that mental play let me create *new stories* for myself, rehearse much-hoped-for but untried ways by which I wanted to live my life. I populated my mental world with imaginary and very real heroes and heroines. I created a loose, imprecise composite of desirable traits, attitudes, and outcomes. Admittedly my parents' virtues (which were plentiful) conditioned my ambitions and perspective.

Although our home had its share of serious problems — ill health, for instance, and both financial and emotional upheavals — moral and ethical excellence was not lacking. Virtue, in one form or another, was a key, central value in our small family circle, as was creativity; and I craved these diverse expressions more than food.

From a wider mix of information and observances than my immediate surroundings could supply, I adopted a wider mix of future possibilities. Quite consciously I used books, movies, the lives of family friends and self-told stories to add hope, new ideas, and a larger context to my own life. (No doubt *all* children's natural tendency is to use their minds in this inventive way — and youngsters with "street sense" all the more. They would probably manage more beautifully if not coerced away from their best instincts by the socialization process or by unthinking adults and institutions.)

I didn't like the tales my parents' lives told, although I loved them dearly. Moreover, hearing their stories — watching them live — I despaired. I wanted more life (for them *and* for myself), not *things* necessarily (and . . . yes, I also yearned for things), but actual livingness: joy, a sphere of creative authority or vital presence and — for me at least — freedom in what I sensed were my special areas of talent. What healthy person, especially in childhood, doesn't want all this? I bridled at the helplessness of youth, all the while, energetically concocting ways to competently cut new patterns from the cloth of my life. This was bold, serious work and it kept both inner and outer demons at bay.

As I describe, in this and later chapters, after gaining a certain high-quality soundness of emotional health (somewhere along the road to self-realization), it is entirely possible — perhaps imperative — to reinvent ourselves and life's circumstances for the better. Here is when fresh stories help us shape the life we prefer. Ones that we create or ancient tales that we revise for our current needs seem equally useful.

My childhood's mental play — admittedly at times born of desperation and at other times of joyful self-discovery — proved to me that stories unfetter life. Carolyn G. Heilbrun comes at all this better than any other author I've read. She says that it's *only* through stories that we learn to make up our lives:

> What matters is that lives do not serve as models; only stories do that. And it is a hard thing to make up stories to live by. We can only retell and live by the stories we have read or heard. We live our lives through texts. They may be read, or chanted, or experienced electronically, or come to us, like the murmurings of our mothers, telling us what conventions demand. Whatever their form or medium, these stories have formed us all; they are what we must use to make new fictions, new narratives.[8]

Elementary themes, not necessarily complex or serious drama, can transport us from over-intellectualized, linear, unfeeling states to a softer experience of our shared human condition. Even the shortest story brings insight when viewed with objective awareness. Some idea in the author's mind communicates with some need or inquiry within ours.

The Nescafé TV commercial — called "The Blind Date," I think — is a picture essay of a leathery, middle-aged cowboy who's "starting over." The story depicts a mature man's boyishness as he prepares for a date. In the opening scenes he's polishing his boots and self-critically examining his weathered face in the mirror. His adolescent daughter enters his room, bearing comfort: a cup of steaming hot Nescafé, of course. Now roles reverse — she's his consoler and empathic cheerleader. The generations unite. Apparently when it comes to romance, all of us ride around in the same embarrassed boat.

As a result of seeing this two-minute essay on the awkwardness of dating (and the blessing in caffeine), I imagine many middle-aged, newly divorced or widowed people remind themselves that, once again, they must sustain a kind of youthful self-consciousness in order to satisfy their higher needs for mature relationships. With insight, self-study, and ongoing reflection, practically any story contributes its morsel to our scramble of useful ideas. Out of tidbits and trifles, we invent a more abundant life. This too is spiritual.

Incubating Your Own Creative Enterprise

As a young adult I persisted with sober playfulness at this restructuring of personal reality.* But many people — especially adults — are severely handicapped in this matter of making up new stories for themselves. They think small and blandly. They are unsure of themselves. They have been educated away from their creative impulses. Like Claudia Draper, they can't separate fact from fiction. They live for the approval of others or have never "played" with

---

*The insights from these musings led to my formulation of Positive Structuring, the method I've outlined in my book, *Developing a 21st-Century Mind.*[9] Briefly, Positive Structuring is a way to alter one's inner and outer realities, improve life for the better. This way is simple but not always easy. The technique has three broad phases but few other rules, and I used the broad outlines of Positive Structuring in designing the protocol of Chapter Seven's activities. This method seems an effective tool for personal change as it allows us to create new stories for the enhanced life we want.

reality. Perhaps their inner world — hunches, dreams, bits of spontaneous, strong feeling — frightens them. Whatever the cause, their minds lack elasticity.

By contrast, healthfully creative individuals of all ages and types find great, easy enrichment in their own diverse ideas, visualizations, and mix of experiential and constructive projects. By this rich combination, artists, entrepreneurs, gifted scientists, and probably even the "average" guy down the street *invent* their next steps and life-solutions. Such people are, to me, spiritually gifted — especially when otherwise stable and effective.

Film is a *perfect* vehicle for the gestation process required of all such creative enterprise. Movies are but passageways to our own visual, reflective, and nonconscious experiences. Cinema is fast moving, like our minds. It initiates a reverie of sorts — not to be confused with passivity or hypnosis. Movies speak in pictures, symbols, fantasy — this is the language of our minds. Our daydreams, dreams at night, and any reading, research, or turnings of ideas along a given theme let us combine not only film but *any* art (and all related data) into an unconscious incubation stew. The richer this mélange, the more likely that we'll produce a creative synthesis of hoped-for answers.

Playing With Ideas and Images

Many people intuitively receive much food for thought from their film-viewing. They do so without conscious effort. Almost all my friends admit that movies — on television, video, or in theaters — help them unwind, explore or invent answers, and identify meaningful personal goals. For instance, one entrepreneur I know scoffed when thinking that I meant only "fine film" enables self-improvement:

That phrase "fine film" is limiting and elitist. *Any* movie can awaken something special in almost any person. Even TV — that supposed cultural wasteland — helps me.

Every Sunday night, I watch reruns of that series *Quincy* or I look at one of the Sunday night movies to get set mentally for the upcoming hectic workweek. I can't articulate exactly what film I need to watch, or why, but I know it when I see it. Movies stimulate my creativity. I watch them to regain a particular state of mind or to re-create an attitude, say courage or boldness. It's time to acknowledge how powerful this medium is in all its variations.

A husband and wife team work together as business partners. They regularly save Friday nights for their movie viewing. They go out alone (minus children or friends) to an early, five o'clock show, then have a quiet dinner at a restaurant. Their habit is sacrosanct. She says,

> We choose movies that we both like and that stimulate our talks together afterward. This is how we unwind, get ourselves ready for the weekend or return to intimacy and romance after a competitive, pressured week. Our friends know better than to ask us out, or intrude, on our Friday night movie.

A young man who described himself as "in recovery" uses films to learn about his next steps in therapy. He said,

> Therapy taught me to pay close attention when I'm moved by stories, art, or a chance remark. So, for instance, when *Crocodile Dundee* affected me deeply — made me feel simultaneously safe and invigorated — I reflected on it. Dundee seems to be an idealized version of the father I wanted, but never had.

I saw I want to develop realistic aspects of the traits he [Dundee] had: an ability to be available to others, courage, self-confidence, and self-protection skills. It's a kiddie-flick. So what? I learn from everything.

Another young person, shy and inhibited as a teenager, told me she used movies to improve her social adroitness. By studying movies, she taught herself how to act on dates, at parties, and on job interviews.

Insights pop into awareness when we take time to day-dream. Such reveries let our mind incubate many possible aspects of our objectives. Watching movies is one way to activate the positive irrationality of our unconscious. Films legitimize our own fanciful, futuristic, or improbable scenarios. They also provide a socially sanctioned way of what friends call zoning out — our dreamy, soft engagement with both our conscious and unconscious faculties.

If, say, after researching a goal as best we can, we put aside this initial, quite logical task and do something entirely different, like read, swim, sleep, watch a film, then largely subterranean mental functions go to work. These combine rich assortments of this or that piece of a possible answer. While we are occupied in some other way, our hidden mind fits together diverse fragments of our puzzle. From this simmering subconscious amalgam comes insight.

Many men say that they get their most useful ideas when they're shaving — not when straining to find elusive answers. The inventor Tesla discovered a self-starting motor as he recited one of Goethe's poems and, simultaneously, watched a sunset. Somehow the combination of *hearing* the poem's rhythmic phrasing coupled with *seeing* a red sphere settle into the horizon was a sufficient admixture to trigger in Tesla's "logical-mathematical, spatial linguistic and musical mind" a blended synthesis that resulted in his invention.[10] The Nobel prizewinning physicist Richard Feynman thought "synesthetically" whenever he had an abstract problem to solve:

> I had a scheme, which I still use today, when somebody is explaining something that I'm trying to understand: I keep making up examples...the mathematicians [come in with a terrific theorem] and they're all excited. As they're telling me the conditions...I construct something [in my mind] which fits all the conditions.[11]

My own way, which I've described in my book *Developing a 21st-Century Mind*, matches this. My best answers come when I'm looking the other way. I like to visualize, hear, feel, and touch diverse bits of data — from across varied disciplines — as a way of constructing answers. I create a lavish mosaic of input and information. I *build* composites of ideas. I actually construct tangible projects (i.e., I remodel rooms, gardens, tear out walls in homes, etc.) as one favored way of manipulating abstract concepts, giving them concreteness. This activity somehow *structures* solutions in my mind.

It is usual for one such project to stimulate multiple understandings, again crossing over numerous disciplines and issues. Stories on film are a perfect adjunct to my meandering, idea-hatching process. Movies let me order and synthesize a kaleidoscopic assortment of unconsciously stored material. Dr. Vera John-Steiner's research into creative thinking clarifies this phenomenon:

> ...the thought activity of greatest importance is the pulling together into a whole — the synthesis — of bits and fragments of experience, which the thinker had previously known as separate.[12]

Perhaps because of its animation, sound, color, special effects, and seemingly endless representations of reality, movies provoke imagination and also stir up, then sort, the symbolic codes and files within our mind. As noted, film's picture-language matches our own unconscious one. A lovely alchemy between logic and illogic results, again, *if* we use film selectively and with prudent, creatively intelligent judgment. The Rig Veda states that mind is the swiftest of birds. Movies help our mental processes soar as they are meant to. To determine how films have guided your imagination, ask yourself

- How have films helped me regain lost confidence or hope and what types of movies accomplish this? When have movies reminded me of the reality principle?

- What films, heroes and heroines, or *types* of stories have mentored or guided me toward my best self and away from that in me which is destructive, hurtful, unfriendly to life?

- When have movies given me lasting lessons or some positive shift of mind and heart or enabled me to relinquish something in a way that, ultimately, opens me up to a larger, finer quality of life?

- When have relationships in movies taught me something about my own human connections, my life in community, my availability or, perhaps, lack of intimacy with others?

The Impulse to Transcend Life's Limits

More than seeking solace for my childhood's absurdities and losses; more than wanting freedom from any restraints inherited from what has been termed a "female destiny";

more than needing to make money or win friends and influence people, I struggled — even in adolescence — with an artist's press for self-expression. Life, Truth, and God were unfolding in my skull. Does not this same impulse exist in each and every human skull?[13] Are we not all artists of a sort — straining to transcend life's limited forms and obstacles to express something fragile, lovely, and mysterious?

Nikos Kazantzakis compares the force and power of this urge to a "gigantic breath — a great Cry which we call God."[14] He says that *all* humanity is tormented by this Cry: "Were it not for this, our world would 'rot into inertness and sterility.' "[15]

It sometimes happens, especially if we've been hurt or oppressed, that we suppress our bid for life. For instance, some children and adults feel *guilty* for wanting more — more love, more virtue, more life. If this is so, then the study and exercise of virtue, suggested in the following pages, is the *best* — perhaps the only — means of restoring our dormant spiritual nerves and holy, neural pathways. To study virtue from a textbook could, for some, be dry as dust. Movies, on the other hand, offer plentiful, exciting lessons, all the more palatable since these are embedded in generally splendid entertainment.

Films are rich sources for learning about virtue — and about life itself. Our own decency lets us, once more, hear and openly heed our inner, silent Cry. Kazantzakis is a comfort, suggesting that when we call out in despair, " 'Where can I go? I have reached the pinnacle, beyond is the abyss.' ...the Cry [will] answer, 'I am beyond. Stand up!' " When movies give our heart — our inmost mind and eyes and ears — the conceptions needed to stand up, be certain: we held these fine sufficiencies within, all along.

 **3**

You know what the secret of life is? ...one thing: just one thing. You stick to that and everything else don't mean [anything].

[What's the one thing?] That's what you got to figure out.

—Curley
City Slickers

AWAKEN INNER STRENGTH

Those who wished to understand [Zen] came to the master, but the latter had no stereotyped instruction to give, for this was impossible in the nature of things. The point was ... not to understand what came to them from the outside, but to awaken what lies within themselves. The master could not do anything further than indicate the way to it ... there were not many who could readily grasp the teaching....
—D. T. Suzuki, *The Training of the Zen Buddhist Monk*

A client of mine (whom I'll call Jane) said *Tootsie* stimulated her own humor and native playfulness. Jane was not referring to matters mystical, just describing how fresh insight revived her dying career. Jane, a talented, assertive woman, was naturally effervescent, a born leader. She felt stymied by her management's empty promises of job advancement. Jane presented her concerns to her manager, the vice president of her division, who seemed put off by her forthrightness. "He told me that I should be patient, a good corporate soldier."

Around this time, Jane saw *Tootsie*, "Not for any deep, psycho-spiritual reasons," she added later, "just for fun." Something about the movie haunted her.

Hoffman's character was so vital and alive. I hated the female lead. In her, I saw myself: a simp; passive, weak, and infuriating.

As I watched, resentment bubbled up. I'd been such a "loyal corporate lieutenant," I'd buried the real me. Tootsie's feisty nature showed me what I used to be and want to be: myself — bold, inventive, and unafraid.

The following week, Jane's dreams vividly highlighted her apparently suppressed desire to be and achieve more. In one dream, Jane was cleaning all her windows: "I needed to see out as far and as clearly as possible." In another, she found lost coins, rare stamps, and other precious valuables ("...my own worth and power, I'd say"). Subsequent dreams contained humorous sequences of her maneuvers around company red tape and pomp. One morning she woke up laughing, "My dreams that night were a hoot! Something in me obviously enjoys a challenge."

Jane's consciously digested admixture of film, dreams, and personal reflection resulted in regained dynamism. She quickly corrected her work concerns.

I'd lost direction and my sense of humor. *Tootsie* gave me a jolt. My dreams showed me that I have leadership options *if* I keep my eyes open.

Instead of being a passive, dress-for-success book-end, now I say what's on my mind. My memos are hilarious; some of them even get answered in the same tone. For better or worse, I'm visible again and certainly less paralyzed.

Whenever fear subsides, whenever alienation lessens, we approach our own special genius. This genius is unique, our most virtuous self — that state of mind and heart when we experience, as Thoreau described it, "life nearest to the bone and sweetest."

Our dreams, fantasies, and desires invite us into these unknown reaches, our private inner landscape. As Jane indicates, so do fears and frustrations. Although we're endlessly entreated to this secret, shadowy region, it is usually closed to our conscious mind. When and as we are ready, stories from real life, literature, from myth and art help us uncover our own concealments. Cinema animates this covert life — prompts holistic insight, lets us examine what otherwise we suppress or fear as alienating and forbidden.

Who knows why we prefer one movie over another? As with books of a type (mysteries, spy thrillers, or historical novels and nonfiction), when a filmmaker's imagination connects with some favorite phantom of our own, magic happens. When we were children, and still capable of make-believe, we simply *entered* various pretended realities with a kind of sideways knowing.

Dismantling Resistance

Let's look at Henry Hobson, that selfish, closed-minded widower in the 1953 British film, *Hobson's Choice*. Henry has three vivacious daughters to support. He hopes to marry off two, but self-servingly believes that Maggie, his eldest, is "beyond marrying age." She's thirty. She has spunk and self-styled assertiveness. The movie's sharply defined darkness, not just its classic black and white tones but also Maggie's lack of contrition when facing her father's tantrums, her keen mind and her ability to work and love productively — creatively — evoke shared memory. Maggie's quest for freedom and dignity reveals a common human experience far beyond my ability to articulate.

Maggie is bright and efficient. She's become Hobson's

domestic, his business manager and — for all practical purposes — his substitute wife. Temporarily she's boxed in yet never servile. Insensitive and coarse, Hobson (Charles Laughton) insults and exploits Maggie as his due. He can't imagine any man finding her attractive but won't let her go. Lack of imagination and total absence of empathy, insight, and delicacy are only some of Hobson's intellectual deficits. He's bright, but his affective IQ is nil.

The ambitious, enterprising Maggie knows exactly what she wants. When she asserts herself and finds a husband, Hobson becomes enraged. Maggie opposes him on all fronts and succeeds. Hobson cannot swallow the obvious: His world order has collapsed. People (represented by Maggie) are no longer his private property. Only with illness, as death's door opens, does Hobson's mind turn grudgingly toward affection and new possibilities for life.

Many of us are Hobson. We too live under the sway of biased, obsolete, or rigid thinking. We thwart and abuse the Maggies around us if they aren't tough enough to stop us. In the 1800s, Hobson's choice was whether to exist harmoniously with others. Today we face (and often resist) precisely the very same option. It can help us scrutinize our unyielding nature (or applaud our heroic tenacity if we're like Maggie).

Nearly too late, Hobson learns his rigidity is life-threatening. For one thing, it discourages acceptance of self-and-other, an active, "let-it-be" posture. For another, his closed mind is loveless; engages in circular intellectualizing — frequently an escape hatch for any real communication.

As the bullheaded Henry Hobson demonstrates, an archaic, narrow mind — the old view — reinforces what is psychically unhealthy. Yet somehow, to us, a narrow mind may seem self-protective. Our tendencies to do battle with our relatives, our petty irritations, or foot-in-the-mouth diseases distance us from people, keep us safe (if also un-happy and, like Hobson, alone). Here again, bit by bit, memorable movies like *Hobson's Choice* dismantle tough walls of resistance *if* we watch with an open inner eye and personal connectedness.

Studying Melodrama

Melodrama is ripe with possibilities for spiritual or psy-chological self-study and discussion. Author Marcia Landy suggests that melodrama follows life. It reveals a "constant struggle for gratification and equally constant blockages to its attainment."[1]

Self-actualizing adults tend to function *through* their personal melodramas — not always, but usually. It is not that these individuals don't feel or suffer, but they actively work at living against the tide of their unproductive, mech-anistic, or life-avoiding strategies. Like Maggie, they're aware of — and move toward — what they need, value, and want. This knowledge adds tremendous power to their behavior. Self-actualizing adults strive for objectivity. They aspire to extend their limits and break through what has been called "hallucinations of imprisonment." Maggie could believe her father's opinion of her — could adopt his biases against her. Instead, she boldly ventures forth, creates her own life as do all heroes of mythic proportions.

The contemporary film *Cross Creek* teaches us about this real achievement. The movie takes a soft, reflective look at personal, creative transformation. It is supposedly a story about author Marjorie Rawlings' writer's block, after which she wrote *The Yearling*.[2] Mary Steenburgen plays the refined novelist relocating from sophisticated city life to a backwoods southern everglades. She's gentler than Mag-gie; her obstacles differ, yet not entirely. She knows she must stimulate and strengthen her literary powers, add power to writing that is bogged down with excessive romance and too little authenticity. Here too, a central figure shows us vision, demonstrates inner calling, a sense of what she must do to live fully.

During the months of her self-imposed isolation we watch the delicate Steenburgen living, serious and monk-like, in a tiny spartan cabin. She maneuvers around desolate marshlands in a leaky boat, gets distracted by romance and volatile, intimate friendships, yet plods ahead with her writing. She *functions*. Knowing what she is. and what she must do, helps her. Over the course of this story, as fear and self-doubt lessen, we see a genuinely fine writer come into being. Despite rejected manuscripts, dwindling funds, and emotional upheaval, Steenburgen persists. She tames her unproductive nature and finds creative rebirth as a result. The reality principle here is that, with strong intention, we too can renew our creative sensibilities — regardless of circumstances, predisposition, or conflicts.

To grow spiritually, we must build capability. Perhaps we lack the requisite character, physical strength, tenacity, or intention to achieve our goals. We may quit (or collapse) under the weight of normal day-to-day pressures. We may waffle about our ambitions and, variously, stand in our own way by skirting any true commitment. This is life-avoidance, our recoil from responsibility. Ill health, mounting expenses and unpaid bills, job frustrations or marital problems can easily derail any of us. If we allow it. Even social slights and subtle insults are sufficient triggers, causing our dispirited switch of loyalties toward the negative. Then, instead of our long-range, most meaningful life-purposes, we concentrate on our bad feelings or bruised egos.

Everyone knows what it means to be undisciplined in their use of energy or talent. This tendency keeps us mediocre, suffering and responding in a slavish, unfocused manner. In my low moments, when I'm stubbornly resisting work, growth, or denying some unnameable fear, movies like *Cross Creek* or *Hobson's Choice* resonate with familiar overtones. Once I recognize the truth — even if foggily — my bogus stuckness dissolves. All this is a matter of degrees. The question each somehow eventually asks (and no doubt answers, if only silently) is, *"To what, over the course of my life, have I been faithful? What predictably gets my time, attention, and love?"*

Understanding Your Identifications

Until it nearly kills him, Henry Hobson serves his lesser self — comfort, manners, and possessive sensuality reign. Perhaps, like Henry, so do we. When asked what we really want, we answer, "I don't know." As the renowned psychologist Fritz Perls once taught, "I-don't-know" usually means "I-won't-tell."

When we cannot, or will not, develop the tools to move beyond what is now popularly and too glibly called our *wounded inner child*, we forfeit our inherent potential. We continue to hurt, to blame parents, work supervisors, or friends for obstacles that block our success. But *we* are the barrier. *We* exchange potential inner strength for a tortured existence. *We* substitute the words "virtue," "character," or "personal responsibility" with the despondent concepts and vocabulary of self-defeat and misery, defining ourselves with symptomatic phrases like "chronic fatigue," "abuse," and "burnout."

Whatever our individual story, virtually all our actions and discussions erode confidence. We abuse ourselves, are subservient to a Hobson-like, inner spirit. This adds to our victimization, ineffectiveness and, ultimately, our sadness.

We live desperate — but not necessarily quiet — lives. Our inner Maggie adopts "our Henry's" verdict, forever.

One can hardly turn on the news or read a popular magazine without discovering new horror stories about adults who suddenly remember their parents as addicts, abusers, or rapists. Such exposés reveal an ongoing, overt battle, a warring eternal *tour de force* between the Maggies and the Henrys of the world. Acknowledgment of abuse is generally a big step forward for anyone. To listeners, a little verbalization of this goes a long way. With wholeness comes discernment: We can learn when to stop talking.

I'm reminded of a bright, attractive colleague who was roundly rejected from his social and business circles. His "wounded child" narratives overshadowed all other conversation. These sad, self-involved confessions — true or not — were simply tedious. This individual's unquenchable thirst for attention and understanding (apparently forever out of reach) eroded his ability to relate or function effectively. Unlike the movie's Maggie, this person's real life became a sorry public melodrama.

Our melodramas also *silently* thwart our talent and fulfillment. We need not utter one word for others (and us) to see we're hurting and unfulfilled. That we need someone else to explain *why* life is so unfair or miserably hurtful is obvious when our need is constant. Facial expressions, mannerisms, tone of voice, and body language can give testimonies to pain. Both men and women frustrate their "inner Maggie's" bid for power. It is a mistake to think only women submit to domination.

In this matter of silent, sweet suffering,[3] movies have too long painted women as patient, long-agonizing victims. However glamorous female stars seem otherwise, their roles in film, theater, and literature illustrate what it takes to pine away in style. (Even the phrase "growing old gracefully" is meant, I think, exclusively for women, tinged with expectations of how, ideally, women *should* age; God forbid they get fat, get wrinkles, or otherwise "let themselves go.")

Inner Strength Requires Positive Identification

Until recently only the rare film empowered humanity's feminine energies. Rather, "real men" (e.g., John Wayne or Arnold Schwarzenegger) created the fun, excitement, and adventure by taking charge of life or saying "yes" to dreams and achievements.

This historic disrespect for feminine power and accomplishment deprives both men *and* women. Formerly, women lacked stories from which to gain true potency. Even today, women must be diligent hunters to find movies that strengthen them inwardly. Children, the aged, and all minorities are similarly shortchanged, defined as less than heroic, fully virtuous, or whole. (In this, there are embarrassingly few inspired, inspiring films starring minorities from which to draw examples. This is a national disgrace.)

Whether we study contemporary prime time television or review classic films, female leads primarily bravely display loving, suffering tendencies. When women play stoics, victims, or weepers, they accept life's blows, and turn mostly to men for their solutions, protection, or their creative inspiration.

In TV's *Dallas, Dynasty,* or the daytime soaps, beautiful, dominant females compete and preen for the attention, approval, and financial support of powerful, achieving men. Not until the late eighties (e.g., *Cagney & Lacey* or *L.A. Law*) did TV viewers find accomplished women functioning as a matter of fact — not *after* surmounting some grave tragedy, not after shooting their abusing lovers or spouses, but rather as a natural, commonplace aspect of their overall characters.

Traditional stars (like Bette Davis, Joan Crawford, Greta Garbo, Jane Wyman) taught us how to bear up under the strain of insults, rejection, or repressed inner potential. To be loved, women practically had to be saints — and ornamental ones at that. Occasionally, a Mae West, Myrna Loy, or Katherine Hepburn playfully, assertively, demonstrated competence and spirited independence, but not as the norm. After all, The *Thin Man* series featured the shrewd prowess of a male detective. His droll, helpful wife and darling dog were but amusing sidekicks.

Only recently have strong, functioning female detectives appeared on prime time television (e.g., Jessica Fletcher, *Murder She Wrote*) and in the movies. Viewed unconsciously, these older films jaundice our self-opinion. Pam Cook's fine article in *Imitations of Life* suggests that, in movies, the woman's viewpoint has been depicted as paranoid, hysterical, or hallucinatory:

> The woman's ability to see is frequently questioned; she may be literally blind (*Magnificent Obsession*) or blinded by desire (*Spellbound*), or lost in a world of shadows and uncertainty (*Rebecca, Suspicion*). Her desire is often presented as a symptom, resulting in mental and physical illness (Joan Crawford in *Possessed*, Bette Davis in *Dark Victory*) so that her body becomes an enigma, a riddle to be read for its symptoms rather than an object of erotic contemplation. This hysterical body is inaccessible to the male protagonist, often a doctor or psychiatrist who fails to understand it adequately, to explain it, or to cure it (e.g., *Three Comrades*). Thus it threatens to slip out of male control, and the only solution is frequently the heroine's death.[4]

Hallucination, as I mean it, is a human, not a gender, problem. Stories about uncontrolled hysteria, the mental or physical symptoms obstructing vital, expressive life, or heroes or heroines with wild, incomprehensible desires turn both men and women into slaves. These undermining themes encourage hallucinations and weaken us. The last chapter examines several side issues of this problem, asking you — the reader — to determine your point of view on the matter.

We all have our share of unexamined and erroneous ideas. Some of us think that we can't talk to anyone about our problems. Both men and women swallow or internalize their feelings. Others *overtalk* their concerns. Men and women of all ages and backgrounds routinely drive people away by dominating or controlling them. With wholeness comes our ability to express — and understand — fear, sadness, and anger. We listen to ourselves and others. We join the give-and-take of life or make sense out of what is now irrational. Over time, we effectively resolve negative feelings and get on with the deeper, more meaningful and fulfilling purposes of existence. *This* is what it means to function. Movies as dissimilar as *Alice Doesn't Live Here Any More*, *The Dollmaker*, *Norma Rae*, *A Chorus Line*, or *Birdman of Alcatraz* can help us understand the costs of purposefulness.

Friends of mine lost their only child in a tragic accident. Unsuspectingly, I phoned the husband, whom I'll call Tim, at his office one Monday morning to discuss some business. I could hear that Tim's voice was strained. When I asked him what was wrong, he sobbed openly and told me about the accident. Tim's unvarnished grief was contagious. In short order I was crying too. For many months, whenever we spoke, Tim talked about his daughter and about what he and his wife were doing to recover. As he spoke he wept, saying, "getting this out" eased his torment. Tim went to the office every day — not because he felt obligated:

I'm not functioning at 100 percent capacity. But I *need* to be here. People and my job keep me sane. Day-to-day friendships help me deal with this loss. Somehow I'm gaining strength to face old wounds that need tending.

Within a relatively short time, Tim and his wife felt better. Rather than *force* himself to work for duty's sake, Tim used his workplace — and his colleagues — for his own ends. He did this automatically without guilt or shame for having a human need. Admission of dire pain was Tim's way of connecting to the human community. This helped him heal and get along during a time of suffering. This too — the ability to reach out for what we need — is what it means to function, to live against the tide of unproductive patterns.

By contrast, compulsive perfectionists stoically press on through loss or grief. They suppress their feelings. They've learned to be tough. Often "tough" means treating themselves and others *inhumanely.* They feign stability or hold back tears and generally reject overtures of human warmth. Others so exaggerate their problems' dramatic content that they too avoid reality. Their feelings say, "I'm so special, my discomfort is so excruciating, that everyone must hear each nuance and fascinating detail of what I feel." This is narcissism at its zenith: self-involvement so rich and ruthless that it can, and does, snuff out life.

A tour of the world's mental hospitals and prisons quickly shows us the extent to which improper, unproductive self-expression or rationalization and unreality defeat human potential. Hard work — sheer effort — alone is insufficient for optimal mental health. We all need high, clear, perhaps heroic goals (and a little actual success) to be happy.

True life stories about effective people let us identify productively with others' struggles and triumphs. We project our own worries onto the characters or, in some vicarious way, try to solve our problems along with the heroes. We must not, however, misinterpret this to mean that a movie will settle our inner turmoil or fix some weighty concern once and for all. If it helps at all, it is indirectly — under the surface of awareness, beneath our thoughtful considerations.

It is a sure sign of maturity when we finally reconcile ourselves to the fact that our deepest problems are rarely solved. Generally, we learn to live with these as happily as possible, sustaining the tension that comes from knowing that we don't know exactly what to do. Carl Jung stressed that the purpose and meaning of problems reside in our "working on them incessantly," not simply in finding solutions. This alone revitalizes us, and if we imagine that we've found *the* one and only right answer, "the more likely we'll have lost something."[5]

Precisely because of their animating, sensually imitative quality, motion pictures teach us — as do myths, legends, and fairy tales — how to grow up in this way, how to accept what can't be changed while nevertheless courting self-mastery and meaningful ambition in all joy and gratefulness. Cinema invites our own creative synthesis of insights and responses.

Pictures replicate and then spur a universal play of consciousness. For instance, timelessly, humankind has puzzled over primordial inquiries: should we to stay with something or leave it? what should we do about such-and-such? what is the meaning of life and death? These questions whirl about in our collective awareness — and if they are any good, movies surface and address these ideas.

To be stimulated in this fashion is no small advantage, as any artist or creatively aware person knows.

To revise our life's script from a frustrating melodrama to a mature, resourceful victory, we might judiciously (and over time) immerse ourselves in stories about others who prevail over adversity. If we watch a movie like *Hobson's Choice* or *Cross Creek* as individuals who are larger than a particular age, cultural or racial group, any good tale can be instructive.

No single picture contains *all* our answers (or even most of them). Almost any decent movie raises our unresolved questions. Admitting we are double-minded is the first step to seeding our answers. Again, Bettelheim's remarks about the usefulness of fairy tales are easily applied to film. He explains, in part, how the "seeding" of maturity works:

> The fairy tale...leaves all decisions up to us, including whether we wish to make any at all. It is up to us whether we wish to make any application to our life from a fairy tale, or simply enjoy the fantastic events it tells about. *Our enjoyment is what induces us to respond in our own good time to the hidden meanings,* as they may relate to our life experience and present state of personal development.
>
> ...identification with [*The Three Little Pigs*] teaches that there are developments — possibilities of progress from the pleasure principle to the reality principle, which, after all, is nothing but a modification of the former.[6] [italics mine]

In exactly this fashion, cinema helps us reconcile the tensions in our present circumstances, so that, *in our own good time* (i.e., possibly decades), we modify our personal realities for the better — move from victims to self-actualizers or passive to active causal agents of our own life.

We also project our forbidden hostilities and inner conflicts onto the screen while actors battle their foes. We can examine fictional solutions for insight into real problems. By choosing to identify with substantive, virtuous characters (whether in fiction or real life) or with inept, evil, or impoverished types, we mold our psyches.

Exemplars of Personal Power

In *The Color of Money* a tough, tired-out and streetwise billiard champion, "Fast Eddie Felson" (Paul Newman), makes a comeback by managing his mind and his emotions. "I'm back," he grunts contentedly, returning with full, determined focus to the business of his life. We all know what he means.

Not only Fast Eddie but Vincent — an exuberant, up-and-coming young player — and all those characters aspiring to win at big-money, professional pool exemplify *active* personal power. They possess a tight, disciplined mind and a pool-hall brand of grace under pressure. These qualities flow from pure, objective awareness.

Whether we hope to succeed in billiards, the corporate board room, or family life, objectivity is essential. Fresh, uncontaminated insight, the lucid interplay of interior and exterior cues, activate our most basic spiritual impulse: our wish that life in us surpass itself. The work of integrating fragmented, perhaps despairing or unconscious, bits of ourselves into full awareness is both psychological *and* spiritual. When handled well, this emotional homework results in such improvements as enhanced communication skills and bolstered self-esteem. These traits enable us to grow toward true autonomy.

Form Character; Forget "Perfection"

Films' sumptuous world of images, sound, and movement provides constant, steady commentary about human joy, struggle, and triumph. These lead us through a solitary, reflective pilgrimage to our deepest heart. Here we are reacquainted with our own falsehoods, truths, and aspirations. Whenever films give our mind much needed stimulus to express what is — and has always been — fine and intelligent within, they carry the mystical message.

The movies discussed in this book suggest that characteristics like courage, perseverance, and moral decency are demonstrable qualities in all sorts of people, are largely spiritual traits contributing to our "character." Maggie and Fast Eddie Felson are each distinctive — entirely unlike each other. Nevertheless, they share in common a lavish humanity.

Maggie and Fast Eddie are also imperfect — just like us. Although tainted by all the varied emotions and frailties of our species, they possess virtue and nobility of *character* — that special amalgam of traits equaling valor, honest repute, and an elevated moral constitution. To me their goals seem ordinary. One wants a happy marriage. The other wants to score at pool. What's extraordinary is not their aims but the heroic manner in which they pursue them.

We too can grow in confidence and self-respect as we form good character or learn to strive effectively — sacrificially — toward our ambitions. This means we reach for personal excellence — not an artificial, egoistic perfection.

Movies of every sort illuminate virtue and spotlight the moral elevation inherent in our own souls. When we root for the brave underdog, it is, in part, because we are courageous or have love. When we cry with characters who've been hurt, it is in part because we empathize with suffering, are compassionate and even saintlike. We resist these tender feelings in ordinary life, steeling ourselves against our own or others' vulnerabilities. Films produced mindfully, under the impress of directors' and actors' highest spirits, slice us open with knife-like sharpness, revealing our essential goodness.

Frank Capra knew this. He was particularly aware of virtue when making films like *Mr. Smith Goes to Washington* or his classic *It's a Wonderful Life*. (Perhaps this is why his movies soften hardened hearts.) Even that beacon of sophistication, *The New Yorker*, concedes about *Wonderful Life:* "In its own icky, bittersweet way, it's terribly effective."[7]

We know that Jimmy Stewart's character is fictional. Still, most of us emotionally engage with him, feel some stirring of renewed hope, love, or self-confidence. A brave, heroic performance like Stewart's lifts our spirits, reminds us of our own capacity for truthfulness, bravery, or human affection. This recollection restores power — can infuse us with life — if we stay open.

Positive Identifications Build Strength

All virtues and vices are somehow already ours, although some are dormant within our consciousness. It is easier to embody a trait if we can clearly visualize it. This envisioning is our primary means of learning *any* complex social skill, like walking and talking, like lying or telling the truth. Watching others demonstrate a quality, we imagine ourselves doing so. Over time, imagination dominates our will and intellect.

No matter who we are, it is personally very expensive to express virtue in everyday life. Without concrete examples we can't even comprehend the extent of these costs. Yet films help our imagination calculate the personal risks.

Jesus Christ's rule of thumb on this is so down to earth, so simple: "Which of you desiring to build a tower, doth not first sit down and count the costs whether he have wherewith to complete it?" (Luke 14:28).

When our parents, teachers, or mentors have not demonstrated virtue, movies can be helpful ersatz guides. Certainly we need much repetition and encouragement to exercise our decency. We require virtuous models, particularly if we weren't loved properly — since all of us have a capacity for cowardice or evil. The nightly news bears this out. Paraphrasing Olivia de Havilland in *The Heiress*, when we've been taught by masters we can indeed be very cruel.

I have suggested previously that as we identify with genuinely wholesome people, we construct the scaffolding for our own authenticity.[8] The live, admired model is a blueprint for our mind. Wholeness always demands that we be faithful to new and raised standards of thought and behavior. For optimal personal growth, we must also come to terms with any number of what may now seem foreign or dangerous attributes.

Stories and respected role models are guides that impart information for the enhanced goals or conduct we want. If we are honest observers, we realize that virtue and "good character" coexist with human imperfections. Despite our flaws we begin to feel deserving of our dreams. So comes courage to continue.

No one develops good character without tolerating frustration or casting their nets into the dark waters of the unknown. As we envision leaving our comfort zones, it is consoling to find examples of people whose clear spirits are temporarily, like ours, "puddled by something, [wrangling] with inferior things, though great ones are [their] object."[9]

Here is when an invigorating saga, perhaps like *Serpico*, reassures us that others know what we're experiencing.

(Serpico, Al Pacino, has inspired me more than once.) The wiry, know-it-all Serpico — a street-smart, flawlessly honest, opera-loving policeman — stubbornly defines integrity and good character. We first see Serpico at his graduation from officer's training school. There he sits, bright eyes and mind intent on the commencement speaker's message about police virtue.

> To be a police officer means to believe in the law, to enforce it impartially, respecting the equality of all men and the dignity and worth of every individual. Every day your life will be on the line. Also your character.
>   You need integrity, courage, honesty, compassion, courtesy, perseverance, and patience.*

Not to worry: Serpico possesses all these traits. More important, he is a Believer — he loves this idealized profile, and Mom and Apple Pie and the NYPD archetypal heroics. Instinct tells us Serpico is potentially a super cop. What we don't yet know about him is what we don't yet know about ourselves: Will he have what it takes when the going gets really rough? (Will we?) Can he *live* his highest virtues? (Can we live ours?) How *much* nobility of character is required to surmount the exigencies that life dishes out?

Before he gets his answer, Serpico is stripped bare of safety and friendship, and he's nearly crucified by a profoundly corrupt law enforcement system. His own tough expectations almost do him in as well. Serpico is an endearing — if sometimes irritating — life instructor. He shows us how to "wrangle with inferior things" though great ones are our object.

---

*Worded as exactly as memory permits.

Shocks of Recognition Strengthen

An impeccable performance like Pacino's rudely awakens us to the reality principle. If we immerse ourselves in his story, empathically lose ourselves in it, the harsh requirements of our life reassert themselves. We may discover that we *want* to meet these rough demands. Or not. Properly offended by what we see on the screen, we could summon new energies with which to face our own trials.

The training of Zen monks involves many shocks to the students' minds and bodies. Disciples are hit on the back and about the head if they doze off in meditation.[10] These slaps bring the attention back to reality. In time, aspirants' minds leap to greater understanding and, for some, spiritual awakening. So it is with us.

Westerners seeking spiritual advancement along gentler lines could well consider boosting their minds' leaps of comprehension by pondering the images, symbols, and cues of those qualities that make up character of all kinds. Movies like *A Chorus Line, Babette's Feast, The Heiress, A Man for All Seasons, Malcolm X, Raging Bull,* and *Serpico* can provide diverse, much needed jolts.

Babette's Feast makes obvious in lush, intelligent terms that high intellect blends purity of reason and emotion. To use the vocabulary of *Defending Your Life*, Babette is not a "little brain," although her goodness is uncomplicated. Decency (not logic, not sophisticated debating skill) promotes both her survival and her healing.

Ultimately it is Babette's virtue (multifariously expressed as generosity, kindness, patience, hope, love) that displays her humanity and rescues her from living a victim's life. As *Babette's Feast* illustrates, virtue is not what we do to impress others. It is what we do to preserve our sacred values — our personal aesthetic, the delicate symmetry of our own life, and thus our heroism.

I recommend *Babette's Feast* as an entry point for an initial cinematic reflection on virtue, personal strength, or wholeness and *A Man for All Seasons* for the summation and apex of inquiry into the full flowering of character. Both of these films are, to me, seminal works about the upper reaches of character development, where mature spirituality resides. These movies majestically display the luminous, at root unfathomable, and infinitely variable nature of human goodness. As such, each story speaks powerfully to our intellects — no matter how jaded we may have become. These movies offer clues (from our collective shared unconscious) that spirituality presses us to reach up courageously for final integration. The cry — as Kazantzakis termed our impulse for life and wholeness — reasserts itself, despite difficulties and realistic, painful costs. From Saint Thomas More's life force, from the original author's unconscious, come new structurings and illogical, inspired precepts about how life — our own included — yearns to surpass itself.

Neither *Babette's Feast* nor *A Man for All Seasons* is a chilly, dogmatic lecture or a self-righteous, pharisaical rulebook. These movies — and I would add *Malcolm X* or the Godfather series* — simply prove that, above all, virtue resides in our humanity, our vulnerability — not in our idealized performances, our puny efforts toward perfection, or in our cherished logic. Each movie is a graduate school course on how decent people (to me, larger-than-life heroes) express compassion, courage, integrity, and generosity. Such study is essential if we would be self-respecting heroes in our own eyes.

---

*Coppola's Godfather series is *myth*, not fairy tale, and certainly too vast a trilogy to discuss briefly. This is one of those masterpieces that, like *A Man for All Seasons*, deserves our exclusive attention. For a start, read *The Godfather Films* by John R. May.[11]

Your Meanings Bring Strengths

A story's value is easily ruined if others outline its meaning too specifically. This is certainly true of movies. Films with rich personal relevance may not conform to meanings that others find in them. Our own understandings are intimate partners to our particular virtues — the ones we most need for this or that context of our life. Nor must we avoid paradoxes, contradictions, or inconsistencies. These too — if we comprehend their special messages — can feed our minds with healthful insights.

I love TV's *Mystery Science Theater 3000, Ruby Wax,* and *The Simpsons* but was never moved to see *The Last Temptation of Christ* (although I'm a Scorsese fan). Friends puzzle over this. Similarly, when I was little, I resisted much serious drama yet loved cartoons, comic books, and movies that my refined, urbane parents thought of questionable value. As in close friendships and love affairs, opposites attract. With stories, truly there is no accounting for taste. Nor need we justify our choices. The French proverb "The heart has reasons that our reason does not understand" explains this.

We may love horror films or crass detective tales but loathe violence. We could easily admire certain adventurous characters — 007? Moriarty? Dirty Harry? Thelma and Louise? Auntie Mame? Mrs. Miniver? — but not want to emulate their obviously fanciful lives.

Even children understand that some famous heroes are unreal (e.g., the Tin Man or the Lion in *The Wizard of Oz;* the wicked stepmother in Disney's version of *Cinderella;* or the Ninja Turtles in *Teenage Mutant Ninja Turtles*). Still these might help viewers accept some negative energy (like fear or cowardice) or bring to light long forgotten ambitions, loves, desires, or a longing to be decent. Thus film heroes can promote the reconciliation of feelings integral to wholeness. For this to happen, we must avoid passive, indiscriminate viewing.

Reflecting on the movies that you love, you might explore how these may have helped you accept your flaws or develop your inherent strengths. For example, ask yourself

- What movies encourage me to get out of my own way, intensify my love of life, or remind me that I want to become more brave, more robustly authentic?

- What stories typically promote my healthy functioning (despite unpleasant circumstances or negative self-feelings)? What movies shock me into realizing that what I thought were imperfections were really virtues in disguise? What movies enable me to embrace my flaws — accept myself as I am, warts and all?

- What films stimulate self-awareness or help me feel what I am feeling here and now: anger, fear, hopelessness, resentment? Do movies ever renew my optimism or determination? If so, which ones accomplish this?

- What positive personal traits — like healthy resolve or good humor in the face of unfriendly attack — resurface as I watch selected movies? (Do these films ever stir me to take myself more seriously in some way or remind me that I want to develop some specific virtue?)

- What kinds of heroes or heroines do I routinely and predictably admire? Do they embody typically "masculine" or "feminine" energies? Does my attraction provide information about my own inherent weakness or still-hidden strengths?

This sort of quiet, ongoing reflection seems a natural partner to self-knowledge. Whether we prefer the stories in movies or the theater or gravitate to those in literature or some other art form like dance or poetry, by learning how to strengthen ourselves through stories we wake up, come alive, if only gradually.

4

Don't be too sure I'm as crooked as I'm supposed to be.

—Sam Spade
The Maltese Falcon[1]

FOLLOW VIRTUE

To him that hath, shall be given. And he already hath who has found the riches of his own nature. To find these riches is the first step.... All other things will be added. And to find those riches, use well every talent you possess. Then whatever comes, just be glad. For all things respond to the call of rejoicing; all things gather where life is a song.[2]

—Christian D. Larson

An entrepreneur I'll call Bill used his addictions as subtle entertainments. Bill loved a good chase. Women fascinated him *if* they resisted his charms. Gambling and the fine art of thin-ice brinkmanship were Bill's other favorite hobbies. He enjoyed barely escaping financial crises and time-pressures.

With high animation and lively displeasure, Bill complained of a falling-apart world: a pending divorce and possible loss of custody of his children. But his zest and, more, his obvious pleasure in relaying all of this betrayed him. When I suggested that these excitement addictions might be his unexamined way of avoiding life's responsibilities, Bill laughed. His entire being delightedly recognized (and responded to) the truth.

He admitted that The Chase was stimulating: "Married women and those who play hard-to-get are fun. I doubt that monogamy could be as revitalizing." I asked Bill to

81

watch *Alfie* in this same light. Alfie (Michael Caine), a Cockney womanizer of the first order, is an accomplished hunter of the fair sex. And proud of it. Unfortunately, not until it's too late does he realize that his life is barren. He lacks love and true fulfillment.

By gradually revising his identifications, Bill discovered that work, off-hours' pleasures and particularly relationships were only superficial gambits. Like Alfie, he had traded life's true satisfactions for fleeting excitements. Bill was merely skimming indolently over the surface of his existence. Were he to tackle something deep enough to satisfy his sharp mind, Bill might find sufficient challenge for a lifetime. Yet, such objectives sorely test any of us. In this chapter we explore what it means to risk our all, to fail, to be seen for what we are — perhaps just average. To some this is intolerable. To all it calls for virtue.

Each of us grasps life's crucial spiritual issues in our own complex fashion. Terms like "personal power" or "virtue" are fraught with positive, negative, and cultural innuendos. One friend confessed to me that, initially, she was irritated by my use of the word *virtue:*

> I'd never call anyone virtuous — that's so self-righteous and evangelical sounding. The most I'll give them is that they've done a virtuous act.

Perhaps you also interpret the word as essentially judgmental or as tinged with religious overtones. Skeptics and the sophisticated are suspicious: No virtuous person exists; everyone is corrupt or corruptible; saints are motivated by self-interest. Those less cynical may still consider virtue an abstraction lacking concrete, practical relevance to daily life.

Cynicism and boredom, a preference for evil or for the dark underbelly of experience, and the refusal to take anything seriously are easy ways to block feelings and avoid the tender, painful poignancies of caring, striving, or knowing that something essentially decent lives within ourselves. Early in life, I discovered that almost all my schoolmates joked to break the tension of their own discomfort after seeing a serious movie. They seemed compelled to do the same when someone in the group disclosed a particularly sharp vulnerability.

Too many films portray such crude reactions: Heroes are uninvolved with others' suffering; they poke fun at the vulnerabilities or tendernesses of the helpless. Thus we learn how to deny our own fragilities, our purposeful objectives or our enthusiasms. These movies seem to be the products of mind-numbingly cynical (or unintelligent) directors and producers.

Author Tom O'Brien in describing such crass work says, " ... a deliberately cool refusal to go deep or to credit insights of mind or feelings or heart — to play only at facades — aids and abets all those already strong tendencies in the entertainment world to ... avoid depth."[3] Motion pictures supposedly made for teenagers or young children often lack depth.

The entertainment world reflects us. There is a definite correlation between our collective, psychic impoverishment (at best an immaturity of conscience) and the superficiality of most movies. As individuals, we too skirt the mature, enduring values of life. We want quick fixes, and in the poet Rilke's words "the easiest side of the easy." We too approach life with spiritual and psychological dryness. Certainly we diminish our own humanity — and derail our personal power — when failing to use *all* the means at our disposal to develop, then express, our fundamental goodness.

Even average films talk of what it means to be involved in the tug of war between the abstract concept of virtue and its concrete acts. Heroes and heroines in cartoons, comedies, and of course in most dramas vacillate between cynical and humane assessment of themselves and the world. In *Ramblin' Rose, Lilies of the Field, Pretty Woman, Wall Street*, and *The Americanization of Emily*, we find particularly strong examples of the way ordinary people confront and express virtue. These movies can shed light on our own struggles to be decent or reveal what we value.

Virtue Is Power

Virtue, our fundamental strength and goodness, is no clear-cut black-and-white affair. Its expression is complicated by our life's script — its particular plot, actors, conflicts, and events — and the richness, or special texture, of our unique nature. Some of us are deeper than others. If so, then our intellect and heart *craves* cultivation when we fail to exercise courage, truthfulness, or some other obvious sign of respect for life. Developing these, we'll grow robust, authentic, and joyful — no matter how hard life may then otherwise become. More often than not, such qualities are forged in the crucible of our conflicts, losses, and temptations.

In *Lilies of the Field*, Homer Smith (Sidney Poitier) is an itinerant carpenter, traveling through New Mexico. He happens on a group of German nuns, living in the middle of nowhere. They are new to America, speak little English, and see in Smith an answer to their prayers. The nuns need someone strong and capable to build a chapel for them.

After much resistance, Homer Smith finally surrenders to the nuns' vision. Slowly this small, odd band of holy foreigners becomes Smith's ersatz family. Although we sense

Smith is basically a decent, well-meaning fellow, over the course of this tale he achieves substantive virtue. He yields to the requirements of the job, accepts great responsibilities — even those that aren't really his, and repeatedly turns the other cheek when insulted. Faithfully Smith stays his course, keeps his commitments. However much he yearns to quit, he persists with the building project amidst often inhospitable, exploitive nuns and a community that challenges him. The chapel gets finished and — because of his virtue — Smith also becomes more complete as a person.

Toward the movie's end, as Homer Smith oversees the finishing touches being added to the new structure, we're watching a man who seems to have responsibly finished a key chapter in his life. He is larger, more truly himself, and somehow fulfilled. Smith's character has been shaped by his loving efforts and by the affection that has grown between himself and the nuns.

The simple territory of this tale depicts how virtue assumes a human shape and proportion. The reality principle is repeated: Our inherent positive qualities are gained largely through struggle, hardship, and mature dedication to something larger than ourselves. This is an evolving, unending matter.

The movie *Wall Street* shines a subtler light on human goodness. Here virtue is less obvious. We must look long and hard (beyond the primary characters' debased lust for money and things) to find it. The film is played out on a wide, contemporary landscape where money and power tempt, corrupt, and eventually betray Bud Fox, an ambitious young stockbroker. Unlike the more patient Smith, Fox (Charlie Sheen) is in a frenzy to exchange his working-class heritage and values for those of Wall Street. He aims at a glitzy, mid-eighties' definition of success. Fox is speedily seduced by a charming robber baron. His mentor, Gordon Gekko (Michael Douglas), has the Midas touch, and Fox willingly tarnishes his own innocence during his short, stressful apprenticeship in avarice.

Wall Street's images tempt us as much as power and wealth entice Bud Fox. The movie inundates us with symbols of luxury, chic and all those fabulous things money *can* buy: lavish penthouses; designer suits, state-of-the-art kitchens, luxury cars; leather and chrome corner offices; power over others. We too may covet these. We may even hope Fox makes it big (who doesn't want the American dream of success?). But Fox can't have phenomenal success without phenomenal personal costs. Neither can we. The reality principle returns.

Fox pays for success with his virtue and his relationship with his father, whom he adores. Ultimately Fox's basic decency wins out when he must choose, once and for all, his loyalties. (Of course, the fact that he gets caught in an ugly, insider-trader scam helps him see the light.)

Many of us are impaled by our own ambitions. Perhaps we're working toward conflicting goals. Or we're torn between opposing ways of behaving: We want success, yet need virtue and love — much as we need air.

Working Girl, Big Business, and *The Secret of My Success* are other contemporary films that likewise, in comedic fashion, reveal the pitfalls of excessive ambition. Stories about people who must struggle to behave decently can illuminate our answers or show us why we're hurting. While a movie does not give us *the* solution to our problems, a good tale sticks with us, highlights various options, lets us *feel* our truths and virtues (which we may otherwise ignore).

Virtue Is Uncomplicated

Nor need we make this too complex. Even young children know what virtue is: *The Simpsons'* little Lisa Simpson and her mother, Marge, are virtuous. It's obvious; it's simple. Their kind, compassionate natures, their generosity, all that they say and do demonstrate a basic sweetness, self-respect, regard for other people.

Homer Simpson knows what truth and virtue are, yet his flesh seems particularly weak. Homer can't behave as his conscience dictates. He usually struggles very little and gives in easily to temptation. (Just like us?)

Then there's Bart: and he's a whole other story. Bart voices our universal contrariness and acts out our dangerous, disruptive desires. Bart has a demon living in him (fairly close to the surface of his awareness). Bart gleefully throws marbles on the floor when he knows someone in authority is about to walk by. Perhaps that's why we laugh: a demon lives in us too.

Author and ethical theorist Jonathan Jacobs suggests that virtue is "the most complete operation" of our powers of personal agency. Practicing virtue is uniquely enjoyable because it makes our life intelligible and affords us "maximal exercise" of causality:

> ... persons typically enjoy and find worthwhile the exercise of their agency. Its most complete operation, virtue, yields the richest and most stable type of enjoyment ... the more fully one's causality determines actions and dispositions, the more fully able the agent is to understand [these]. Being moral can make a decisive contribution to having a coherent, lucid personal narrative.[4]

Our virtue is our finest, most trustworthy means of experiencing the vibrancy of personal power. The greater our direct expression and direct *experience* of virtue, the higher is our quality of life, health, joy, and inner peace. Movies can help us touch this inner core, this life-source, although of course they cannot provide experience itself. Most motion pictures made for children (e.g., the old Charles Dickens's classics or the recent Disney hit, *Beauty and the Beast*) animate the value and practical benefits of virtue. They can induce insight in people of all ages.

Movies cannot whisk us into a state of permanent goodness. For that, we ourselves must activate intelligent imagination and develop our own courage, honesty, resourcefulness, and patience. A friend expressed discouragement about his inability to actualize his long-term goals. Desperate to succeed (he's studied every available self-help program), he can't seem to erase the imprint of childhood's pain and helplessness. "The people around me — my parents, old friends — were and are habitually negative. I've not had encouraging, uplifting mentors to help me pry loose from self-defeatist tapes." His focus is off kilter.

Few of us have had ideal, nurturing parents. (A probable reason why almost everyone idealizes other people's childhoods while decrying their own.) The reality principle is clear: We must pry our *own* attention loose from self-defeating tapes. In real life, no one does this for us. Films can prod us on, providing frameworks for productive ways to be and behave. *Alice Doesn't Live Here Any More* or *Breaking Away* tug at any existing emotional umbilical chords of viewers of all ages and backgrounds. No matter how simplistic the picture, our psychic wrenching is hardest when we're still unhealthfully wrapped up in (and choking on?) deathly old scripts or suffocating ties. Conscious assent to wholeness requires an altered world-view, a shift of *both* our focus and our behavior.

Motion pictures are contemporary mythologies, modern versions of folk and fairy tales. Like scriptures of every culture, these aid our sorting-out process; they let us commune with something alive and healthy in us that persistently cries for release. This primal, underground communion activates positive and life-supporting values, ideals, and remedies, deleting past defeats and impotence from memory.

As scripture teaches, all other things are added to *whatever* images we store in our minds. Therefore we would do best to saturate our awareness with themes of hope, virtue, and triumph. Perhaps one reason that serial movies like *Star Trek*, *The Terminator*, *Lethal Weapon*, and the *Rocky* sequels are so captivating is that these help millions feel vicariously powerful. In an era when growing uncertainty, fear, and helplessness are pandemic, films that reconnect us to our positive, personal powers may be healthy and necessary.

Virtue As "No-Strife"

If you observe your own nature when you are perfectly calm and happy, you will find what I call "no-strife." This perfect balance seems an extraordinary zone of peace — a perfect detachment, open to all. This is, I suspect, our most virtuous state: the point of entry to so perfect a humility and love that we are at one time both full and empty — aware of all-encompassing, incomprehensible mystery, yet unaware of "self."

There are times when we feel complete, desire*less* — we have everything we could possibly want. At the same time our egocentric or social self disappears in a kind of perfect harmony or humility. For example, people often say that when they release their hold on some weighty problem, they find peace of mind and total acceptance of the inevitable. This peace is no-strife.

When we fill with wonder at our insignificance within the general scheme of a mysteriously grand and wondrous universe, this too is no-strife. Perhaps we're looking out over the edge of the Grand Canyon, or scuba-diving, or walking along a white-sand shoreline, bordered by miles of aquamarine ocean: At such times self-consciousness subsides and awareness shifts. We are present. Our *is*-ness is enhanced. Initially, we think *little* of ourselves; then we don't think of ourselves at all. "We" disappear. This too is no-strife.

Peter Sellers' character in *Being There* embodies no-strife, if only in a caricatured fashion. He plays Chauncey Gardener — a simple gardener, abruptly ousted from his job at a secure, protected estate — who becomes a national celebrity because of his uncomplicated, organic philosophy. It is unfortunate — for my descriptive purposes as well as for the formation of collective consciousness — that Gardener is an intellectual and emotional cripple. Few films properly illustrate no-strife, perhaps because there is nothing dramatic about this state of being: Gardener charms us because he just *is*.

No-strife is an experiential instant in time as well as an impetus to ongoing transfiguration. For most adults, living in industrialized countries, even the notion of a *moment* of such perfect calm and happiness seems out of reach.* Many people cannot conceive of inner peace and are far from able to observe this state to discover for themselves what, if any, benefits it might deliver. They are so thoroughly scattered by overcommitments to work, money, or family that merely considering a slower pace depresses them — it seems so unattainable.

---

*The film *Grand Canyon* beautifully depicts this state at its conclusion.

No-Strife Takes Practice

The Buddhist precept "what you do, do that" is a key ground rule behind the various practices used to enter our mind's inner calm — the silence of no-strife. Academic training and high achievement, however beneficial, do little to help us gain no-strife. No-strife demands less (not added) mental commotion and far fewer (not more) complicated theories. In this, *The Terminator* — who blasts his way out of trouble — is passé.

We best approach pure awareness by *practice*, not by intellect. Shunryu Suzuki, a spiritual descendent of the great Soto Zen lineage, enumerates the discipline of such a practice. It involves

- mindful concentration on everyday tasks (not simply courting the peak or ecstatic instant)

- single-minded "right-effort" that does away with idealized over-exertions and prideful ambition

- selfless, non-attached giving

- constancy, present-centered emptying and an available, here-and-now focus

- practice (rather than intellectual debate).[5]

Our upsets, opinions, illusions, and pet fictions distract us from who we truly are. These block our promise, keep us struggling and servile. Our diversions are, shall we say, stimulation agents — the powers we employ to keep ourselves emotionally stirred up. Internal noise or agitation is the commotion of human life.

The great Hasidic scholar Martin Buber wrote that these preoccupations confuse us with a thousand memories and "interrupt every pure, beautiful astonishment" of existence.[6] As we relinquish commotions we step into a new consciousness of enhanced spirituality.

Sister Lee Agnes, an author and spiritual retreat leader, wrote in *A Taste of Water* that she is happiest when not thinking about herself. Ordinary people — not just make-believe characters in movies — can practice this:

> [When I forget myself] I have no anxiety about the past, no present worry, no anticipation about the future. I am simply in the very flow of life. This is when I really enjoy life.[7]

We practice no-strife whenever we concentrate fully on a task, an object, or the present moment. Some call this "mindfulness." In time and with persistence we forget ourselves. As we consciously exercise clear, non-judgmental thinking, or — as Homer Smith did — press through hardship so persistently that, as individuals, we are elevated, our choices invite feelings of gratefulness.

We experience increased poise or a sort of dynamic gladness about what we've accomplished. These are quiet satisfactions, deep fulfillment, not hubris or self-pride. Such directions stem from a mature personal completion — a true integration of our core self into every level of our being — final integration with the deep things of existence.

People who write to me about my book on right livelihood say that when working on tasks suited to their minds and bodies (or, conversely, when they transcend ill-suited jobs), they feel on the one hand strong and innately powerful, and on the other, as if they have lost themselves. They vanish into the activity — become completely one with whatever they're doing.

However brief, time spent in such self-forgetfulness introduces keen, sharp thought processes. We appreciate life in all its varied forms. We see that we *are* life, expressed

diversely. Pain, grief, thoughts of limitations or actual difficulty dissolve. Our usually contentious nature rests. We
lack nothing. Like Chauncey Gardener, we are simple,
quiet, because we have everything.

Another movie giving us a look at varying facets of
no-strife is *Harvey*, a classic comedy about Elwood Dowd
(James Stewart) whose drinking buddy and constant companion is Harvey, a giant, invisible white rabbit. Dowd
is a generous, sweet-tempered, middle-aged bachelor who
enjoys his drink a bit too much. Dowd exists in a gentle
reality ("I've wrestled with reality for 35 years, and I'm
happy, doctor. I've finally won out over it.").[8]

By every account Dowd is content and unflappable. He
befriends everyone and genuinely likes people — even his
enemies, such as his older sister, Veta (Josephine Hall),
who is plotting to have him certified insane. Whatever
else we think of Dowd (especially in this age of anti-
alcoholism), we could do worse than adopt his serene,
communal philosophy of life:

> Harvey and I have things to do. . . . we sit in the bars
> . . . have a drink or two and [soon we're talking to
> everyone]. We came as strangers [but we don't leave
> that way].[9]

No-Strife: Bit by Bit Into Being

Brother Lawrence, an uncomplicated monastic who lived
in the 1600s (and who sounded very Buddhist when saying he felt that "useless thoughts spoil all"), admitted that
specific contemplative techniques did *not* help him control his prayers. Physical mortifications also seemed to him
quite pointless. Instead Brother Lawrence devoted himself
to God during his normal daily chores, leaning on God for

the tiniest efforts required to accomplish household chores like cooking and cleaning. Lawrence forgave himself for his failings whenever his mind strayed.

Then, with what he called "little internal adorations" he came, bit by bit, into mystical union with God. "Lord," he prayed, "I cannot do [this task] unless thou enablest me."[10] His modest practice let him empty himself of all self-serving efforts. This is what it means to *practice* a virtue: In the most usual, non-spectacular circumstances we ourselves create the *means* by which we build our decency. The contours and context of our life — relationships, work, talents — are employed to exercise whatever is good in us.

As we practice no-strife, we discover that what *feels* "bad" may contribute to our greatest good. We *notice* what we're doing. The shy person consciously reaches out to others. Extroverts learn to hold their tongues. These are growthful choices although these actions disturb initially.

For instance, a harsh attack on our egotistical tendencies can prod us to reclaim our objective attention, bring us back to our practice. This is precisely when an ordeal can become a consolation, a blessing in disguise. Paradoxically, the path to no-strife often begins with *more* trouble, not less. As we watch our emotions and our body's language, discomfort can point the way to our growth.

Gurdjieff, a legendary Russian mystic, often imposed conscious labor and intentional suffering on his followers. One of his maxims was that we should do what *it* hates. By *it* he meant our usual, conventional self, that in us which craves comfort, approval, and safety. Gurdjieff believed that hardship prolonged life when it awakened us to our uncontrollable habits and separated, self-abusive way of being.

He taught his disciples to "freeze" their habitual postures when, for instance, they were gardening, walking, or dancing. By holding other poses for long stretches of time, they could observe both body and mind and their "very stupid, painful, erotic, fantastic thoughts, feelings, and sensations." Thereby his students jolted themselves into recognition of what they really said or did to themselves. Gurdjieff often achieved the same ends by assigning seekers to jobs they detested.[11]

No-strife also releases new energies. Whereas unconscious habits and feelings erode hope and can weigh us down, our clear unencumbered awareness frees up life's vitality. We feel lighter, happier, and at ease in our own skins. Movies offer us heroes and heroines who grow "lighter, happier and at ease in their own skins." Their acts and attitudes are virtuous and brave. These carry the mystical message.

Virtue and Search for Meaning

Among several provocative themes in *Educating Rita*, the search for meaning is key. Rita's quest for knowledge and a more refined life suggests that personal direction revitalizes our life. Rita (Julie Walters) is a bright young woman, desperate for a college education. Having a blue-collar heritage, her husband and her father hate the fact she's trying to improve her lot. When Rita enrolls in an independent study program in English Literature, her tutor (Michael Caine) finds he's revitalized by this Pygmalion project. He willingly helps Rita undergo a predictable metamorphosis (and *he* changes in the process). She learns superbly. Yet — the reality principle exhorts — neither Rita nor her tutor grow without grave self-scrutiny and, again, steep personal costs.

In one scene, Rita is having a drink with her family at a local pub. Music blares loudly; everyone in the place is singing, drinking beer, and generally having a grand time.

Rita notices her mother sitting quietly amidst the raucous crowd, tears streaming down her face, and asks why she's crying. Her mother admits despair: "I can't help feeling that maybe I could have found a better song to sing for my life."

Often virtue is a force in us longing for more life, better life, elevated morality, or something noble, pure, and lovely currently beyond us. Our basic decency frequently asks us to exercise our good will, to sacrifice comfort as we know it, for far off, invisible goals representing our personal aesthetic.[12] In aiming for these we can easily despair, question our motives, doubt ourselves, perhaps hate ourselves for hurting those from whom we sense we must pull away.

Whatever our age, gender, or background, *Educating Rita* reminds us that courage, boldness, and risk-taking are absolute requirements of a virtuous life. It is not enough to merely think positively: Eventually, we must behave decently, bravely, positively.

Overarching life purposes also become obvious as we leave our familiar setting to express new interests or talents. While engrossed in a challenging career, while dancing, singing or painting, or involved in charitable projects, we know our best self. It is then — just when we forget or lose ourselves — that we find what we've searched for: our goodness, competence, or some deep, sweet joy. John Muir's exquisite sentiments reveal exactly this. Muir, an intimate of no-strife, cultivated this virtue in his own, organic, meandering way:

> I would rather stand in what all the world would call an idle manner, literally gaping with all the mouths of soul and body, demanding nothing, fearing nothing, but hoping and enjoying enormously. So-called sentimental, transcendental dreaming seems the only

sensible and substantial business that one can engage in.[13]

To manage our attention, as did Muir, means emptying ourselves of our usual fretting, gossiping, or restless ways. Observant and attentive to some high, organizing goal or healing element within, we begin to release strife. Thus are we fortified.

Whether we commit to higher education, selfless service, or to a creative project; whether, like Muir, we adore nature or (as Brother Lawrence, Gurdjieff, Martin Buber, and Meister Eckhart) devote ourselves more directly to God, virtue — a wholly new and transfiguring awareness — deepens us and ultimately simplifies life.

Virtue Sees the Folly in "Success"

In *Resurrection*, heroine Edna McCauley (Ellen Burstyn) discovers, after a near-death experience, she has enormous healing powers. People flock to her seeking relief. She quickly becomes a celebrity. The large-hearted McCauley wants to cure everyone, but soon finds herself entrenched in hype and religious conflict. Her success introduces her to a pressure-cooker existence. Ultimately, her own crisis stimulates her wish for a quiet, devotional life, though she is far from traditionally religious. McCauley's notability — an excess of worldly "success" — and her own enlightenment — makes her want a self-forgetful life. This same path is sought by all whose compulsive achievement — like McCauley's — begets inner wholeness. Material success is folly if it separates us from our virtue.

Some of us, like Edna McCauley, are so enmeshed in the business of daily life that we may need to be shocked into doing less. What begins as trauma can end in rare blessings if we follow virtue — persist in its expression. Heart attacks, or bouts with other serious illnesses, financial burdens, or rejection by those we love can force us back to basics, to pay attention to our life.

No-strife helps us focus by simply asking us to respond appropriately to whatever is needed here and now. We stick to washing the kitchen floor despite our boredom. Without complaining, we paint the fence or water our lawn. We *listen* to a friend who needs to talk. This practice has few rules or fixed conditions; no smart systems theories help us. We just give ourselves to whatever we are doing. Practicing no-strife does not mean *denying* stress. Rather we enter fully into the heart of life.

Moonstruck's theme, along these lines, reminds us that the world can trip us up in other ways. Cher plays a young widow who nearly marries the wrong man for all the right reasons. It's time for her to remarry. She wants a home and security. Her fiancé (Danny Aiello) is stable and reliable. Logic tells her this will be a "successful marriage." When she falls passionately, head-over-heels in love with her fiancé's brother (Nicolas Cage) — another person who's hiding from life until love awakens him — the heroine finally summons up the courage to reach for what she needs.

All the major characters in this story — Cher, her mother (Olympia Dukakis), and Cage — assert themselves uniquely in the name of love. There are virtues here. And lessons.

Movies like *Moonstruck* also talk to us about the downside of carrying excessive emotional baggage. We may have been only dimly aware that some of our problems really have nothing to do with us, but we have nonetheless assumed responsibility (and guilt) for them. In a flash of insight we can gain new objectivity. However slight, this lets us put much needed emotional distance between someone else's limitations and our own feelings. We stop taking responsibility for another's upset. (This is no-strife.) Our perspective shifts toward greater equanimity and balance. Perhaps all that changes is our attitude, but something within alters toward greater joy or lightness.

In time, we could even gain the audacity to quietly confront others, saying something like, "You seem to have a problem with this. How will you handle it?" When we hear ourselves voicing plain-spoken objections to unnecessary extraneous turmoil, we know we are becoming more responsible for our own life. This too is virtue.

If we cease *owning* other's unhappinesses, we learn what cheerful individuals have always known: It *is* possible to step out of the way of someone else's misery and avoid leading a dejected life ourselves. Ironically, this emotional distance generates the very insights we want, from which enhanced and workable solutions soon flow. Such heightened awareness and lessened melodrama also build true interpersonal skills: authenticity, effective self-disclosure, and diplomacy (not to be confused with sarcasm or manipulation).

By learning the art of taking care of our own needs, we grow socially adroit. In itself this rare quality improves our chances of being heard. Characters like those in Agatha Christie's *Miss Marple* (played by almost anyone), *Mr. Belvedere* (Clifton Webb), *Auntie Mame* (Rosalind Russell), the butler in *Arthur* (John Gielgud), or *Black Widow* (Debra Winger) reveal the myriad disguises such adroitness could take.

It simply makes good sense, is productive, practical, and liberating to teach others how *we* wish to be treated. This means setting limits for others in how they deal with us and — responsibly — taking the consequences. Movies can teach us "how."

Virtue: Releasing Fear Stimulants

Fear-thoughts can be intense stimulants. We frighten our-selves in our own individual ways. Almost all of us have worried about the things we dread: financial ruin, health problems, or some other potential horrors.

With these chronic, anxious notions we prop ourselves up when we're bored or unchallenged. We may use anxiety to motivate ourselves toward greater worldly achieve-ments or reinforce our masochism and thus keep ourselves off balance. We excite ourselves with such thinking to spice up an otherwise dull and meaningless existence or to prevent ourselves from sloughing off. Students who wait until the last minute to write a term paper often frighten themselves into last-minute studying.

Children use horror (e.g., tales of ghosts and scary — to me, obscenely violent — stories like *Friday the Thirteenth*) as a means to outgrow their fears. (So do adults.) Movies that pit good against evil are fairy tales helping young people face their worst nightmares. Steven Spielberg's contempo-rary classic *E.T.* is wildly popular with children, in part because of Spielberg's genius at sustaining tension between good and evil in fresh, surprising ways.*

Almost any movie (even television sitcoms) can help both children and adults desensitize themselves to terroris-tic *inner* visions by their repeated immersion in the fictions of the very thing feared. Humans rarely tire of fanciful sto-ries that let them face loss, the unknown, hardship, fears of abandonment, anger, and punishment. In our minds we re-hearse and resolve a thousand events that never take place in actuality. Such rehearsal invites growth.

---

*We must thank Spielberg for so generously *reframing* the relationship between humans and extraterrestrials toward loving, peaceful friendship. *E.T.* and *Close Encounters of the Third Kind* amount to a seed-change in consciousness of no small value.

Some people depend on panic for excitement. A friend calls this being a "crisis junkie." She says she's met her fair share of them. No doubt, so have we. Many corporate executives exhibit this tendency.

Movies about virtuous people could lead us back to an ordinary, uneventful life. To crisis junkies like Bill (mentioned earlier) or Alfie or us, the humanizing goals of virtue — intimacy, commitment, or personal transparency — represent a *dangerous* choice.

Full engagement with a vocation or a person (in friendship, marriage, or parenting) requires a slow, tedious investment of steady effort. This obligation puts anyone at risk.

Your Favorite Films, Your Own Virtue

As noted, virtue adopts numerous disguises. Yet uniformly it mysteriously extends our reach, permits our exercise of personal agency and power. Movies can show us our unique path into this effectiveness. In *The Big Picture*, Kevin Bacon plays a young director who (much like Bud Fox of *Wall Street*) is unwholesomely seduced by the glitzy prospects of fame, money, and working at what he loves best — making movies. After experiencing costly emotional and financial losses from unsuccessfully filming other people's stories, Bacon finally risks directing a picture he's had in his mind.

In the film's last scene, his colleagues are amazed, their faces full of wonder and childlike appreciation as they view his finished film, his personal vision. We too may be protecting a fragile, private vision or have some odd but lovely idea about how life might be at its best. Were we to express this beautifully, it too could inspire others. More importantly, by expressing our vision gracefully, we would simultaneously cultivate our own virtue.

When considering how to best express what Goethe termed your "acts of initiative and creation," it helps to reflect on open-ended questions like these:

- What movies predictably renew my vigor, personal power, and willingness to move beyond myself as I am now? What virtues must I develop in order to accomplish this?

- What movies make me hunger for more life, better life, an expanded ability to express some elevated ethic or something I value (but think is out of reach)?

- How have films helped me identify the seeds of success in something I thought at first to be "failure"? Have any movies ever helped me through sadness, personal crisis, or moved me from turmoil to some semblance of regained stability or inner peace (no-strife)? If so, what were they? Can I find a pattern in these?

- What movies would I want my children (or the children of future generations) to view as they develop their life's values and significant purposes? (Try to make sense out of your list to determine how these have affected your own life for the better.)

- What movies would I want shown, studied, and discussed in, say, a prison or rehabilitation center and why? (*If you like your list, consider sending it, and a copy of this book, to your local state prison official or drug rehabilitation center.*)

As it develops, virtue blesses us and makes *us* a blessing to others. It endows us with those qualities our families and communities need: our self-control, inner peace, perseverance, and our kindness. Not all at once, of course, but over time and with practice, even love arrives.

5

It's amazing! The love inside — You take it with you.

—Sam
Ghosts

FOLLOW LOVE

In the end, though, the solution is Love ... And love, it seems to me, implies the realization that perhaps already those subject to us know our failings very well, and accept them with love, and would not dream of holding them against us, because they know these things do not matter. That is the great consolation: in the joy of being known and forgiven, we find it so much easier to forgive everything, even before it happens.

— Thomas Merton, *The Hidden Ground of Love*

Wholeness is a fuzzy, ambiguous concept — hard to define or quantify. Perhaps this explains why the psychological literature so thoroughly details mental illness, yet so obviously lacks words for a notion like wholeness.

Wholeness means robust psychological health, the growth toward authenticity and personal power. We grow whole as we become aware, assimilate and integrate our buried, rejected, unconscious, or fractional selves. The process is unending; self-acceptance and respect for others are natural byproducts of such robustness. We also learn to love, to forgive, and to commit to something — it almost doesn't matter what.

Whole people are not necessarily docile, accommodating, or even "well-adjusted." They don't live according to national polls or popular norms. They are not passive

105

nice-guys, constantly smiling or accommodating us. They actively belong to themselves, strive to be uniquely their own. This is not an easy achievement. Without love — agape; compassion; genuine regard for self and others — wholeness eludes us.

In *To Kill a Mockingbird,* small-town lawyer Atticus Finch (Gregory Peck) assumes the defense of Tom Robinson, a black man accused of raping a white woman. We know this plot spells trouble for everyone concerned. The quiet, self-possessed lawyer is intellectual, a somber philosopher, a widower living with his children in a rural, Depression-era southern town. Atticus Finch takes on the unpopular case despite sensing that a vengeful community and would-be lynch mob could harm him, his two children, and his client. The movie (adapted from author Harper Lee's classic novel) provides one model of the self-actualizing temperament. Atticus Finch shares many traits with other self-actualizing persons, among which are

- a superior perception of reality

- an increased acceptance of self, others, and nature

- increased spontaneity and solution-orientation (as opposed to being problem-centered)

- increased detachment and autonomy (greater resistance to enculturation, the opinions of others, etc.)

- democratic character structure (including improved interpersonal relationships and increased identifications with the human species)[1]

Models for Wholeness and Love

You may be reading this book because you are at a turning point in life: changing jobs or relationships or recuperating from a setback or illness. Perhaps you realize you're living far below your ability level — working at jobs that wear you out because they're too easy, or associating with people whose influence is unproductive or negative. It's possible that you are one of several million adults in this country who have too many problems and too little joy.

It takes hard work to become more of a human being — emotionally healthy and fully integrated. This is especially true for those hoping to express their mature spirituality. Meister Eckhart's lines, " . . . working and becoming are the same. When the carpenter stops working, the house stops becoming," put our efforts in proper perspective.

Research on dysfunctional behavior suggests that wholesome, non-addictive conduct is linked, as suggested earlier, to meaningful self-expression. The healthier we are the more likely it is that we forfeit self-involvement in order to *function*.

When we do our daily chores in an aware, creative, and *conscientious* way, we tend to remain in control of ourselves in other areas. The reverse is also true: If we slough off insignificant tasks or obligations, this is often a sign that negative self-feelings or tendencies lurk beneath our awareness. Later, we may "shoot up" — binge on food, drink, or other habitual dependencies. In other words, our normal behaviors mirror our feelings. And vice-versa.

Our simplest acts predict our futures. These improve (or undermine) our self-opinions. As we grow whole, our *conduct* demonstrates that health. Atticus Finch's example broadens our understanding about what attitudes and acts are required of us as responsible adults. Finch's choices and his demeanor reveal love: for life, for his children, for certain freely-chosen sacred principles that, to him, give life meaning. He is, in all respects, a virtuous individual who embodies strong regard for values such as justice, fairness, and compassion. It is not too much to say that Finch accepts human frailty — his own and others' — as a fact of life. However charming we think we are, without wholeness we feel, along with Waldo (Clifton Webb) in *Laura*, "In my case, self-absorption is completely justified, I have never discovered any other subject so worthy of my attention."

Love: Accepting Shadows and Uncertainty

Dr. Carl Rogers, the distinguished American psychologist, writing early in the human-potential movement, relied on Kierkegaard's phrase, "To be that self which one truly is," when describing the aims of those with psychological health. This means such people *learn* to welcome whatever is authentic in themselves — their flaws and virtues, their strangeness and strengths, the big and little shadows of their secret self.

Even when these dark energies are less than flattering to an idealized self-image, a maturely loving person succeeds in resolving the paradox, feels warm regard for self and others. Atticus Finch reveals just this type of maturely loving person: His inner stance bears close inspection.

Rogers also observed that, as his healthiest clients neared wholeness, they actively strived for autonomy. They enjoyed answering life's big questions for themselves (e.g., "Who am I?" "What do I value?" "What are my life's goals?" "What's my purpose?"). Again, Atticus Finch models this self-sufficiency. Like Finch's character, Carl Rogers' most robust clients, when whole, struggled to outgrow their facades and pretensions. They sought independence and were self-loving — accepted their feelings, for better or worse.

Non-judgmental self-acceptance is but a prelude to the

wholeness we want. Otherwise it could provide an excuse to continue unproductive or even morally wrong behavior. For instance, we might say to ourselves, "So I cheated that fellow. That's OK, I accept that I'm a cheater." For people seeking self-realization, the point of self-acceptance is merely the first step in new growth.

By *practicing* virtue we cross over significant thresholds of authenticity. We begin using all our inclinations and subselves as partners in actualizing our life. The previously "too-sensitive" individual soon finds that his sensitivity is a higher intelligence of sorts, an important interpersonal screening device — an adaptive mechanism that helps him discern what others need, want, or communicate. The "too-aggressive" person realizes that she uses her dominance to exert control. If she redirects this dominance into enthusiasm — she has an energy with which to lead, influence, or express life.

Expressing these formerly rejected bits of self productively, we grow whole. A host of new inner resources become available to us. We embrace our buried traits or unacceptable energies and turn these toward our creative ventures. If we can just *accept* the fact that we're fearful, compulsive, or conceited, eventually we can stop undercutting ourselves and learn to serve life with these very forces (instead of doing ourselves in with them). Almost any trait can be used to further our best self if we make it a faithful servant to our good.

An aspect of this phenomenon is revealed in the first *Karate Kid* movie, another strong fairy tale reinforcing the reality principle. In *The Karate Kid*, Ralph Macchio plays Daniel, a teenager who's the new kid on the block. Daniel is hounded by a gang of neighborhood toughs and must fight to survive. As good fortune has it, a wise, all-knowing mentor (Noriyuki "Pat" Morita) befriends Daniel and patiently instructs him in the fine art of directing all his energies at a single still point — in this case, his opponent's face.

In his splendid *Film Guide*, movie critic Leslie Halli-well admits that this movie's "...huge commercial success in the U.S. remains mystifying."[2] People usually like a film when they see themselves in it. Most of us long to harness our mind's deeper powers. We intuitively know there's more to us than meets the eye. Like Daniel, almost everyone is plagued by fears or nameless anxieties.

Our contemporary culture provides us with a sobering obstacle course: rapid change, economic uncertainties, and the added demands of new personal roles may seem like bullies. Any of these problems can do us in if we're un-skilled, incompetent fighters. Then too, Daniel's enviable relationship with his teacher is archetypical of the loving, good parent/child union that everyone wants (and that al-most no one has). Through trusted, enlightened friendship Macchio's character grows stunningly, expertly capable of focusing his inner powers against all outer foes (instead of being crippled by these).

I repeat: We can view even simple films as stories about deeper, human issues and qualities rather than identify with these narrowly as race, culture, or gender narratives. A movie about any small subculture can be studied in its larger, universal context. This is fortunate since few movies exist with the images and metaphors to help di-verse viewers — minorities, the elderly, etc. — develop their uniqueness.

For instance, we can watch *Baby Boom* as a humorous portrayal of comedian Diane Keaton coming to her senses *as a whole person* — not simply as a woman.

Initially, Keaton's character is a fast-track, self-reliant executive, obsessed with success. She's working herself into an early grave. When she inherits a baby, Keaton is a typical Supermom who tries to keep everything going smoothly. For this single parent, there aren't enough hours in the day to efficiently tend to the hearth and the corporate profits. Alas, realistically, her boss faults her when family demands lower her finesse and productivity.

When Keaton retires to a picturesque farm, as work pressures subside, her ever-more vibrant, entrepreneurial powers are unleashed, and she becomes a self-made millionaire in yet this second arena. Author Tom O'Brien called *Baby Boom* "nearly worthless,"[3] but fatigued executives everywhere (and not just women) will identify with Keaton. The reality principle in this movie — as in life — is that we hurt ourselves when trying to make everyone happy.

A movie must be specific if it is to reach us. Overly abstract, preachy stories are thin, charmless affairs. Still, while watching movies about women executives or male bartenders, we can translate particulars into broad-gauged terms, "read" a film as we do poetry or novels, find metaphors and symbols of good and evil, joy or frustration, success and failure in *any* plot.

This is not complicated — not at all like suffering through a dreary homework assignment. Rather, this conversion from individual to universal elements is an automatic, empathic reflex of spiritually mature minds. Children easily accomplish this.

City Slickers is most obviously a man's film — practically a men's movement picture: Three ordinary guys, friends since boyhood, experience a kind of early, middle-aged crisis en masse. Mitch (Billy Crystal) is nearly forty and depressed about it. ("Did you ever reach a point in your life where you say to yourself, 'This is the best I'm ever going to [look, feel, and do] and it ain't that great'?"); Phil (Daniel Stern) loathes his loathsome wife ("If hate were people, I'd be China."); and Ed (Bruno Kirby) is like a rat in a macho-man's maze — obsessively chasing women and wild adventure to prove his worth.

They decide that an interlude at a dude ranch (what else?) will pump the vigor and meaning of youth back into their dying veins, and they head off for two weeks in Arizona to ride the range. Their plan succeeds, but only because they themselves regenerate their own competence and power as whole persons, "penetrate their daily life with active love." Each man overcomes fear, regret, and feelings of inadequacy by resurrecting his vision and by striving to achieve it.

It is sheer nonsense to assume that only men of a certain age feel powerless or frightened. *Everyone* feels helpless at times. Futility and despair are our shared human condition. Kafka, Castañeda, Kierkegaard, and Nietzsche — among other geniuses — continually wrestled with this one theme in their writings.

Psychiatrist Dr. Erich Fromm suggests that most of us are too psychically weak to sustain awareness of such despair. We hide our truths from ourselves because it is far too threatening for us — "as average normal persons" — to acknowledge such desperate feelings. Therefore, we look the other way, attempt to escape what Kierkegaard called our "sickness unto death." We submit to strong leaders (e.g., as in Fascist countries), we conform compulsively (e.g., as in America's Wall Street culture), or run off with pals to dude ranches:

> [This helplessness] is covered over by the daily routine of [the average person's life], by the assurance and approval he finds in his private or social relations, by success in business, by any number of distractions, by "having fun," "making contacts," "going places." But whistling in the dark does not bring light. Aloneness, fear and bewilderment remain.[4]

Humor is one way to spot our own despairing feelings. What we laugh at in others illuminates traits usually hovering about within — beneath the surface of awareness. If we experience exaggerated feelings (like anger, disgust, recoil) about others, or somehow feel vulnerable as we watch a movie, this too may say that we are close to identifying some hidden, shadowy, rejected aspect of ourselves.[5]

For all their flaws and flatness, *Baby Boom* and *City Slickers* gaily rub our noses (once again) in reality: Less is more. You can't serve two masters. If you focus lovingly, passionately on a single dream, anything's possible — even the recovery of personal power and your life's most cherished purposes.

Wholeness requires commitment, steady focused intention, and pluck. It asks us to examine what we want or what previously we've avoided. Carl Rogers believed that as we grow healthy we assume responsibility for our actions and relinquish our need for safety, fixity, and closure, cultivating a sort of flowing life-process, "an integrated process of changingness."[6] Like Curley — and eventually Mitch, Ed, and Phil — in *City Slickers* or like Macchio's and Keaton's characters, this means we willingly step out into our projects and goals without guarantees of success.

Love Means "No Free Lunch"

The internationally recognized author and psychoanalyst Dr. Alice Miller stresses that genuine emotional well-being is costly. If we truly explore our childhood's pain, we admit into awareness the uncut, unedited version of our young lives.

We might discover, upon looking, that childhood was a time of powerlessness, manipulation, or abuse. Becoming aware of these buried hurts is only a first step to cultivating the mature love that undergirds psychological well-being.

Most people fear looking at their pasts, and therefore deny much that is sad, vulnerable, angry, or abusive. For robust mental health we must acknowledge any remaining rage, helplessness, desire for revenge, and sorrow over betrayals.

Although as adults we may still long for loving, wise parental attention, most of our parents were not generously attentive like Atticus Finch. Our parents had problems of their own. They may have been infantile, or otherwise poorly equipped, to deal with their problems (or with us). As we grow whole, we forgive them — even if we don't totally forget.

Mourning seems essential — not recrimination or blame. It is cathartic to grieve for lost, lonely years or our own lies. These behaviors, like self-acceptance, restore aliveness and regenerate humanity but are not instant, easy accomplishments. A superior level of mental health gives us the courage to face the past, to forgive, to feel what we feel at present, and to get on with life effectively.

Only then do we proceed with the work of our own authentic life. This too calls for courage and personal power. Miller reminds us there is always more to do:

> [After therapy has been completed] it is up to the patient whether he wants to live alone, or with a partner; whether he wants to join a political party, and if so, which one...his life story, his experiences and what he has learned from them will all play a role in how he will live. It is not the task of the analyst to "socialize" him or to "bring him up" (not even politically, for every form of bringing up denies his autonomy), nor to make friendships for him — all of that is his own affair.[7]

A loving, trusted relationship (as found in *The Karate Kid*); a warm, enduring marriage; deep and constant affection for a child, friend, or family member — all these and much more can work therapeutic magic. At first, healing comes by being loved, by having a good, stable, selfless parent (e.g., Atticus Finch). Eventually, it is not so much the love we *get* that reconciles us, makes us whole, but rather the love we give.

A New Leaf tenderly illustrates how this transformation and turn-about happens to one ambitionless, self-indulgent man (Walter Matthau). In this story, a loveless, aging bachelor has squandered his considerable inheritance on sports cars, custom clothes, and riotous living. Desperately afraid to work, Matthau plots to marry a rich woman so as to murder her for her money. ("I don't want to share things, I want to own them all by myself.")

Enter Elaine May, a botanist — his intended victim. She's generous and kindly but totally inept. Although brilliant, the stereotypically absentminded professor is so socially regressed, so clumsy, she can't dress or feed herself correctly. May's character is also a pushover for her thieving hired help.

As the two move awkwardly through an assortment of newlywed experiences, we watch Matthau *growing up*. Love works its mysterious alchemy in his psyche. From the start his wife trusts and adores him. Both individuals benefit from this.

Long months of caring for her somehow touch Matthau too. Paternally, he inspects his wife each morning before she goes to work. He cuts off dress tags that hang from her new clothes, or wipes bits of egg yolk from the corners of her mouth. Soon he's expertly organizing her financial affairs and firing her disreputable household staff. Responsibility (i.e., one of love's disguises) strengthens Matthau. He finds talents and skills he never knew he had.

In addition to its "work improves your character" theme, this sweet tale underscores another reality principle: Compassionate love (given or received) softens the stoniest heart. Love raises self-esteem (both May and Matthau bloom) and seeds lasting emotional health. By movie's end, an endearing scoundrel is reformed. (He's even agreed, with May's steady [maternal?] encouragement, to become a history professor.) True love is established and the pair live happily ever after.

Solitude and Autonomy

In *Living Happily Ever After* I suggested that three critical factors help us accept an otherwise unacceptable past. These allow us to investigate our personal history with objectivity, and, eventually, to build solid mental health. First, we need *positive self-value*. Certainly this quality, over time, can come with competent, caring therapy or (for some) with prudent self-study. Second, *learning resourcefulness* leverages what we currently know into new, untried areas of effort. Finally, we need a *strong drive toward autonomy*. None of this is a quick-fix.

Too many of us lack and want encouraging support systems. We have not found a mentor like Miyaji in *The Karate Kid* or a model of tough authenticity like Curley (*City Slickers*). We may feel alone and vulnerable. Yet a hallmark of wholeness is that we *want* to proceed on our own. We relish our independence.

Autonomy and aloneness (not to be confused with rebellious loneliness) are purifying elements, much sought-after luxuries we instinctively crave as we move toward self-realization. Much of this coming into our own as authentic persons entails our doing "psychological homework," as outlined above, like the dismantling of old myths.

Here is when we need inspiring new stories, language, and symbols as metaphors and frameworks for our healing or moving-on. Stories that provide us with heroic motifs and patterns reveal ways to re-create life's adventure and then live this with a renewed mind.[8]

Thanks to the VCR, one new aid to self-knowledge is the great library of videotape movies so easily available. When love is the sub-text of the tales that we ponder, both our unacceptable and acceptable features are easier to embrace and express.

All this (the undoing of previous fictions, the emergence of skills, the finding of our true purposes — the whole enchilada) demands patience, tolerances, and *self*-compassion. The gaining of vibrant personal power comes not from hurdling over some single, finite obstacle. Nor does such power increase if we try to "know ourselves" in merely a conceited narcissistic way.

Reel Power entails watching movies in an objective cogitating way, with objective self-criticism. We're disentangling ourselves from illusions, making sense and meaning out of our lives, learning how best to live, and finding out to what one, superordinate *thing* we would devote our life — how to invest our life with active love.

Life's big questions include determining our overarching purposes: Where do we fit into the scheme of things? How do we productively relate to others? What do we hold sacred? And what on earth (or out of it) do we believe?

Movies viewed reflectively, talks with trusted friends about some of these issues, short-term therapy or spiritual direction can help us find our own answers. This means we'll know the kinds of heroes and heroines we have *in* us or the story that we want to live. Slowly, slowly, as

Gertrude Stein wrote, "the history of each one comes out of each one."

We elevate our self-opinion as we recast ourselves in healthier, lovelier, or more courageous roles. (I can't fathom why educators and community activists haven't yet utilized the good lessons in movies when attempting to elevate youngsters' self-esteem.)

This recasting of life, this heroic retelling of our own story is serious, engaging work. Undertaken over time (perhaps over a lifetime) it builds self-respect. Dr. Thomas Szasz's remark that "self-respect is to the soul as oxygen is to the body"[9] means that as we step forward into virtuous self-creation, we begin living "the good life."

The "Good Life"

I rather like Paul Tillich's description of *the good life:* "life willing to surpass itself."[10] Contrast his definition with the notion of the good life as conventionally transmitted by highly glamorized stories about worldly success, like the movie *Wall Street* or the popular TV show, *Lifestyles of the Rich and Famous*. *Wall Street* posits a philosophy of fulfillment gained through chic and glamorous images, the rewards of amorality and ruthlessness embodied in the smarmy stock manipulator, Gordon Gekko. His line "greed is good" I heard often quoted by corporate colleagues who apparently adopted this new frame to justify their own voracious appetites for wealth and power. Judith Williamson, writing in *New Statesman*, compared *Wall Street* to a slick business tabloid, calling it an "extraordinary eroticisation of money in this sexually troubled era."

The financial flow-chart is the center-fold pinup; looking good is for impressing clients not lovers; keeping fit is about performance at the office, not in bed.[11]

Of course, economic security may help us initially to achieve emotional security. I do not suggest otherwise. Extraordinary busyness, however, is a diversion that only makes us strangers to ourselves and erodes true self-mastery. Films can be guideposts along our way to determining how much is *too much* activity.

Babette's Feast, To Kill a Mockingbird, and *Emma's Shadow* — even *City Slickers* — teach that personal power demands vigorous, conscious engagement with life's strenuous passages. Experience obliges us to develop strength of character, not pumped-up bank accounts. Ultimately, only faithful self-surrender to our life's highest purposes empower us. Bud Fox discovers this for himself when his bid for approval by Gordon Gekko results in personal ruin.

If our aim is to "retrain" ourselves; if we want to function effectively; if we yearn for self-realization in our vocational or relational life; if we would outgrow anger, sadness, depression, isolation, or despair, then as Tillich suggests, our life — as we now know it — must surpass itself, must express its truths. This too is love.

It comes not merely when we recover from childhood's blows and disenchantments but as we actively penetrate our daily realities with our talents, creativity, and the full potency — or truth — of our own humanity. Not an easy agenda. Not necessarily a "happy" objective. Big Daddy's (Burl Ives) speech in Tennessee Williams' *Cat on a Hot Tin Roof* tells it as it is:

Truth is pain and sweat and paying bills and making love to a woman that you don't love any more. Truth is dreams that don't come true and nobody prints your name in the paper until you die.[12]

Self-loathing Resists
Personal Power and Wholeness

When we don't want to understand something, we resist and withdraw energy and attention from it. The topic of human power (i.e., *personal power*) is often an upsetting issue — an issue we fear. We tend to shy away from those truths that say we can be or do more as individuals. Those who loathe themselves, the weak, do not like the fact that they can be strong. Our weaknesses and ineptitude let us remain safe, cozily tucked away in our familiar shells.

Notice the way many of us thwart ourselves just as we start to make progress in our lives. We get bored and quit the very task or employment that handsomely rewards us. We become bashful or flustered at compliments or even the thought of our own merit. We seek excitement in the wrong places — from courting the approval of powerful people to indulging in extramarital affairs, gambling, or other alluring but negative digressions. In this, we all have feet of clay.

It was, I believe, Gandhi who said that people seek rules and regulations to guide every iota of conduct because they don't want to behave responsibly, as they already *know* they should. He meant we dodge — or, at the very least, delay — the inconvenience of our high, fine impulses by asking "how" to develop these.

Our virtue *is* our truest power, and wholeness draws it out of hiding. While films like *Gandhi* and *The Autobiography of Miss Jane Pittman* are much like hagiography (one-sided chronicles of saintly persons), they nevertheless provide powerful vignettes that show how virtue enables potent self-expression.

Abraham Maslow wrote that most of us struggle against the knowledge of our personal greatness. I agree. The thought of displaying inordinate pride or self-confidence may be more distasteful to some of us than honest admission of our strengths or the living out of our "beautiful, brave tendencies."[13]

Many of us here *learn* to deny that we have beautiful, brave tendencies. Our parents may have been stingy with praise, cautioning, "Don't tell that child he/she's done well — that'll result in swellheadedness." (I frequently meet business executives who *crave* compliments but who cannot bring themselves to commend anyone, least of all themselves. Surely they were raised in such miserly environments.)

Almost all of us experience strong inner forces that can (if we consent) separate us from bold, virtuous self-affirmation. For instance, we attach ourselves to toxic forms of work or to the wrong friends or family members. We eat or drink more than is healthy. We squander precious time and attention to compulsive worry and imprint the most banal images on our awareness from soap operas on TV or violent films, undermining ourselves with base and negative ideas.

We are fortunate when the pinpricks of conscience awaken us to what the American philosopher John Elof Boodin called a "hidden instinct for unity."[14] No less a man than Saint Augustine was grateful for inner discomforts. These ultimately turned his life around and led him to spiritual completion:

...by inward goads didst Thou rouse me, that I should be ill at ease, until Thou wert manifested to my inward sight...by the smarting anointings of healthful sorrow was [I] from day to day healed.[15]

As in the films described in these chapters, "healthful sorrows" arrive in varied forms: illness, divorce, the pain of some public humiliation or error. Like Augustine we too can be thankful for *any* goad that helps us see we've strayed from our life's true purposes. Our despair becomes an opportunity in disguise.

We can use whatever comes along in the service of self-realization, no longer striving for grandiose objectives or merely to be comfortable. Whatever our station in life, with character we discover that *who* we are has nothing to do with either pain or pleasure. This, taught the Zen master Ying-An, is much like perfecting an art like archery: "...eventually you reach a point where ideas are ended and feelings forgotten, and then you suddenly hit the target."[16]

Virtue Empowers Us

I'm not alone in stressing that, from the earliest of times, those who *live* their authenticity are threatening to others.[17] Individuals who follow the dictates of their conscience are generally ridiculed or rejected (or worse) during their own life. Later, they may be hailed as heroes.

Sir Thomas More, to cite one example, lost his life when he would not bless his king's marriage (Henry VIII). More was beheaded for his act of conscience. *A Man for All Seasons* clarifies the hazards of making waves.

Despite the fact that ultimately More was acknowledged a saint, we must not cut ourselves off from him by believing that he was prissy or somehow inhumanly great. He is our brother — a true kindred spirit. Of him, playwright Robert Bolt generously says,

> Thomas More, as I wrote about him, became for me a man with an adamantine sense of his own self. He knew where he began and where he left off, what area of himself he could yield to the encroachments of his enemies, and what to the encroachments of those he loved.... What first attracted me was a person who could not be accused of any incapacity for life, who indeed seized life in great variety and almost greedy quantities, and who nevertheless found something in himself without which life was valueless and when that was denied him was able to grasp his death.[18]

In the final scenes, a commoner enters center stage to discuss the beheading with the gathered townspeople. He's also addressing us, his audience, saying, "I'm breathing.... Are you breathing?... It's nice, isn't it? It isn't difficult to keep alive, friends...just don't make trouble — or, if you must make trouble, make the sort of trouble that's expected."[19]

Finding what makes life worth living is risky business. It implies that once we know we must seek it. Otherwise we will hate ourselves for our avoidance. If we don't, life will be valueless. Here is when virtue (what Western scripture terms "fruits of the spirit": patience, charity, gentleness, and, most importantly, love) strengthens us for the long, heroic haul.

Virtue allows us to dare to define what our life must be. Virtue bolsters us. And not a few do find their highest purposes, even with the obvious risks. Nothing has changed. Curley (Jack Palance) — the leathery, tough cowboy stereotype of *City Slickers* — is a virtuous man: He's committed. He risks. He's invested his life with active love and meaning, even though he's without family or friends. That's why his example inspires the three lost friends.

As in More's day, the majority prefer the safety of not knowing and stay out of trouble by remaining dull to what, in them, is life, has meaning, gives value. (Frankenstein's remark "I've been cursed by delving into the mysteries of life!" may be our own secret point of view.)

A Man for All Seasons energizes and empowers us (when we're ready) precisely because it tells us of someone strong enough to express his truths, his moral goodness, purity, and fine, clear intention. As Galatians 5:23 puts it, "against such things there is no law."

Nothing in this world prevents our cultivating such power and nothing in this world can stand in our way once we possess it. Heroic stories of mythological proportions help construct our faith in this and build strength where we are weak.

A Greek word for virtue — *dunamis* — exactly encompasses the concept of wholeness I'm attempting to convey: Virtue is personal, divinely inspired power.[20] We know we are empowered when we're able to stay the high ground, our consciously chosen life's course, despite obstacles.

In Mark 5:25–34, we read that a woman who had been hemorrhaging for twelve years was instantly healed merely by touching Jesus' cloak. The woman approached Jesus in a crowd. From all we know she hadn't spoken to or been noticed by him. Yet when she touched him he knew immediately that virtue — power — went forth from him (v. 30). Her presence was known to Jesus only after this force was drawn out of him.

Again, in the Gospel of Luke (6:19 and 8:46), *virtue* and *power* are used interchangeably. Here too, Jesus addresses another huge throng. Everyone flocks around him, wanting to be healed of disease or cleansed of their "unclean spirits" by the power (or virtue) that flows from him. Moreover, Jesus tells the healed that it is *their faith* that has special drawing powers; it attracts or pulls power from God.

Stories heal. Their teachings can awaken inner strength, nobility, and self-value. Myths and fables ignite and dignify life. Our favorite movies are emblematic of ideas we need and value for this enrichment to happen. While engaged with these, we sense what we are at our best and comprehend what we must do to act on what we know is real and meaningful.

Your viewing patterns pinpoint the traits or images you intuit you need. Think back to the movies and books that you love (or to historical or family folk tales, etc.). Which heroes and heroines do you most admire? Which tragedies, dramas, or comedies evoke self-loyalties or compassion?

Gradually your characteristic, unique interpretations, and your personal relationships with stories might come to light by mulling over questions like these:

- What stories stimulate my awareness and expression of added dignity, goodness, or other specific virtues?

- When, if ever, has a particular movie moved me to some improved *action*? (If several movies have positively impressed you, describe the type or tone of these.)

- What can I learn about myself (or my life) from films that are turn-offs, which sadden me or fill me with inordinate feeling — perhaps so much emotion that I cannot continue watching? (*Note:* Don't force yourself to sit through movies that you don't like. Instead, *try* to discover what irritates, angers, or bores you. Keep in mind that your inquiry is personal; you don't need to justify, explain, or even understand all your likes and dislikes.)

- What movies encourage my best sides, make me "a better person" — kinder, more considerate, or friendlier toward others? What sorts of films negate my finer qualities, fill me with fear, anger, or ignoble tendencies? Which of these films do I naturally choose and what do I sense this means?

- How might I "use" movies to develop my virtues, to strengthen what I already know is worthwhile and positive in myself? Might I find a few like-minded friends with whom on a regular basis I might meet and discuss the self-development aspects of movies?

 **6**

[Before you learn to punch]
better learn balance. Balance is key.
[If] balance good, Karate good.
[If] Karate good, everything good.
[If] balance bad,
better pack up and go home.

—Miyaji
The Karate Kid

FOLLOW BREATH

It is not wise to rush about.
Controlling the breath causes strain.
If too much energy is used, exhaustion follows.
This is not the way of the Tao.

—Lao Tsu

Businessmen tell me that after attending a few Lamaze classes with their pregnant wives they manage everyday stresses better. One young man said that after the breathing classes he grew self-aware, saw that in highly charged, competitive situations like corporate meetings or even when alone watching football games, he'd clench his jaw and fists.

I'd hunch up my shoulders and crouch over. I didn't really breathe at all. By staying conscious of my breathing, I've lessened a lot of unnecessary strain.

This chapter explores an effortless practice that promotes self-awareness. I call it *following breath*. It involves the imperceptible, objective observation of that inmost carrier of life: our breath. By quietly noticing our breath as we watch movies (or, for that matter, do anything else), we slowly learn what most Lamaze practitioners know: Our own breathing is a fine teacher about our states of mind. Following breath is a technique that stabilizes us when we're off center. This is good news, since all the world's sages and cultures agree: Equanimity — emotional groundedness — is our healthiest, most potent condition.

While the phrases *following love* and *following virtue* imply ways to study a movie's spiritual content, *following breath* suggests a manner of being, a mode of heightened awareness that lets us experience ourselves, keeps us present. In time we may want to transfer this practice to other activities, like high-risk meetings at the office or routine family discussions. Practiced properly, this delicate, discerning process shines light on tensions and avoidances, and gradually reestablishes us in right relationship with ourselves.

Physiological Fine-tuning

Breath is our most intimate stress detector — a high-frequency, physiological fine-tuning device that amplifies our body's slightest changes. Breath's language is subtle and responsive. Its rhythms alert us to anything faintly out of the ordinary; disruptive thoughts and feelings, minute external sounds, add movements. Our breath tells us when our energies turn into fear or excitement (two closely related states) or when anger, sorrow, and even pleasurable emotions like joy or profound love move through our body's intricate passageways. Breath is an organic, living miracle.

Our breath is us, consciousness itself — the primal source of what the ancient Tao Te Ching calls "the ten thousand things." The Bible's creation story bears this out. The Book of Genesis says that the Lord God made humans and breathed into them the breath of life, after which "man became a living being."[1]

Breath is the obvious causal link between mind, body, and life. This is why following breath and restoring health-ful breathing — easy, deep, natural — makes practical good sense.

Usually we're unaware of our breathing. Perhaps this is as nature intended it. Yet, when we don't know what we feel or where in our physiology our breath, energy, and emotions sit, we've taken things too far. Beginning in infancy, all but a fortunate few realize that it is dan-gerous (perhaps forbidden) to know and express their full range of emotions. Gradually, off-centeredness — and funny breathing patterns — result. Numbness becomes our preferred state of being. This is also when various denials and projections begin.

By pushing our feelings and insights deep down into unawareness we anesthetize ourselves. We stuff our nat-ural fear and curiosity (two completely spontaneous reac-tions of all sensitive, creative children) into some hidden, secret place. Over the years, with constant repetition, we forget what we've done with these, disassociate ourselves from our own perceptions and experience, and in the process, learn to distrust ourselves.

Our nameless, "illogical" fears, our disgusts and avoid-ances, as well as exaggerated awe and admiration of selected others (e.g., parents, teachers, bullies, sports and popular heroes, movie stars) provide clues about our pro-jections. A common sense, rule-of-thumb is that the more intense our fear, hate, or idealized opinion of someone or something, the more likely it is that we've placed some self-rejected power onto another.

The renowned psychoanalyst Dr. Karen Horney be-lieved that children's submissive reactions (also their non-responsiveness) send clear messages to adults, namely, "I repress myself because I need you." Conversely, youngsters who protest or who express strong emotional reaction court trouble (e.g., strenuous battles with authority figures); they own more of their power and breathe better than youngsters who bottle up frustrations, irritations, and their softer, sweeter sides. Childhood submissiveness demands unhealthy self-restraint.

To live in society we need personal control, must internalize social rules, learn politeness, the art of accommodating others. Submissiveness is excessive self-control, the counterproductive, cripplingly severe suppression of feelings, opinions, or values.

We overdo control if we believe ourselves to be inadequate. We then behave like wooden blocks, think we can't make a difference in our own life, subdue our voices, hold back exuberance, energy, ideas, *and* our breath. These we bind up somewhere in our body as tension, anxiety, awkwardness, or chronic pain. This strangleholds our natural intelligence, particularly creativity.

We can see repressions in our dominant, persistent moods — apathy, our chip-on-the-shoulder attitude or severe resistances, especially toward authority figures or our best interests, or in our constant cheerfulness. Our pervading disposition carries a message. The always-tidy, perky woman or the ever unctuous nice-guy generally give away power, as do introverts who *try* to live according to artificial rules-of-togetherness, or extroverts who tiptoe quietly around the expectations of others.

In all likelihood we trust our manner of emotional restraint, however it's fashioned, while feeling ashamed of our spontaneous instincts. We may believe the former are helpful, strategic allies. True, these did protect us when we were tiny, helpless beings, most in need of love, approval, and security. Since we're still alive, our various defenses did contribute to our early life's "success."

In our psyches, we may have encoded rules like, "Be nice — it's safer," or "My repressions pay off." In part, this explains why it's so frightening for some of us to voice our true opinions or to protest (even when — logically — as adults we know we have every right to express ourselves, that there's nothing to fear). As we dissolve those learned responses that thwart our spontaneity, express appropriate aggression, or release stored feelings of laughter or sadness, we increase competence and our power as authentic, whole persons. On this issue F. S. Perls wrote frequently:

> The awareness of and the ability to endure unwanted emotions [was] the *conditio sine qua non* for a successful cure [i.e., of neurosis]. This, and not the process of remembering [i.e., one's traumas or disturbed past] forms the *via regia* to health.[2]

In simple English this means spiritual health depends on owning our own power.

Following breath unearths much that we've buried, particularly our unassimilated experience. One hallmark of neurosis is that we forgo *self-consciousness* for *self-awareness*.[3] When self-conscious we project our eyes and minds outward, as it were, into others' ways of seeing and thinking. We exchange *our* values, self-expectations, standards, and opinions for theirs. As if in a giant *Mother-May-I* game, we stop reaching for our deepest goals if others don't approve.

Then we forget our ambitions, lose sight of life. People who can't figure out how to spend their leisure time or who wonder what careers to follow often suffer from this malaise. Following breath increases our endurance of the previously unendurable: once hard to accept self-affirming ideas (e.g., that we are competent, causal agents of our life). We slowly reintegrate into our self- or world-view.

Not for a moment do I suggest that merely watching films, in and of itself, solves long-standing problems. Nevertheless, the stuff of our repressions and imperceptions does become the unfinished psychological business of adulthood. To *see* clearly, we must regain fresh, uncontaminated, *whole* sight[4] — receive realities that exist beyond our programmed prejudices. Movies, and our breath's varied reactions to their messages, can show us our biases and can pinpoint the way to our healings. Initially, we simply stay present and alert. One way to accomplish this is to follow our breath. We watch our responses with interested detachment.

Given what we know about society's enculturation process, gaining whole-sight is not easy. Diane Cappadona's article, "The Art of Seeing," describes seeing as a transformative discipline. We're made new through vital, visual encounter.[5] Noting how our perception is shaped by previous experience, Cappadona suggests we consider Kierkegaard's story:

> Once upon a time, there was a man. As a boy he was strictly brought up on the Christian religion. He had not heard much about what other children commonly hear, about the little child Jesus, about the angels, and suchlike. On the other hand, they showed him all the more frequently the Crucified, so that this picture was the only one he had, the only impression of the Saviour. Although only a child, he was already an old man.[6]

While following breath does little to train the *intellect's* sight (i.e., does not help us compare visual nuances in film to the compositions and symbols in classic art), the technique is subjectively revealing — can potentially develop pure awareness, that "ideal condition of the psyche that... is the aim of meditation and [which is] the source of a healthy individual."[7]

One friend told me that when she saw Danny Glover's portrayal of an evil manipulative man, she stopped breathing:

I was amazed at my reaction to Glover. Apparently I'd adopted this habit [of holding my breath] in childhood when a sick, sinister relative cared for me. The movie brought back all my terror.

Following breath spontaneously improved matters. Every time she noticed herself holding her breath, she would naturally sigh or yawn, thereby drawing into her diaphragm much-needed oxygen. Her friend Jay watched the same movie alongside her, yet experienced no such problem. She described Jay's reactions:

He yells at the screen whenever he's agitated. I realized for the first time how healthy this is. All during the movie, whenever Glover's character seemed especially cruel or mean-spirited, he'd spout off. Plus, Jay didn't understand why the family in the story allowed the cunning Glover to remain in their home so long. I never questioned that — just passively accepted Glover's presence.

Ask "Who's Projecting What?"

Studying a movie in this fashion, we learn much about our own tendency to relate lopsidedly to circumstances, to see people through a rigid, judgmental, emotional filter, and — as Jung described projection — "without possibility of doubt."

A close study of a popular film like *Thelma & Louise* helps summarize all this. On the face of it, this female buddy film is simply an updated, feminized version of the traditional all-male fable. We've all seen bonding, coming-of-age adventure films or mystery thriller classics (e.g., *Easy Rider, The Sting, Lethal Weapon,* even *Diner* and *Rain Man*) that paired males whose mutual affection deepened during the saga and was endearing.

As with the films listed in Chapter 7, *Thelma & Louise* lets us observe the mind, or consciousness, with which we watch movies.

1. *Before viewing:* Familiarize yourself with the plot, the characters, to get a sense of your immediate reaction to the story.

Thelma (Geena Davis) is a naive, long-suffering Arkansas housewife. She has tolerated her crude, truly despicable husband as long as possible. (Watch for the signs of her progressive victimization. The precursors are all there: Darryl, her idiotic husband, ignores and discounts her. He scolds her like a child, bullies, and intimidates her.) Their domestic interactions may trigger heavy feelings — irritation, helplessness, or anger, depending on your predisposition. As you watch, notice your breathing, especially when Thelma pretends *not* to notice. What happens in you as she suppresses her rage?

How do you feel later, when, predictably, Thelma erupts violently? What is your response to Susan Sarandon, her waitress friend? Is she healthy, prudent, and intelligent? Does she seem a realist to you? Are you disappointed when their "weekend vacation spirals downward into an alternating hellish nightmare and black comedy? How do you feel when Sarandon's control unravels?

2. *While watching:* Try to locate love's energies, and virtue, as these deepen your interest in the characters. (Each film differs in its handling of such qualities; just

as each day offers us varied expressions of love and virtue.)

Do you experience Thelma and Louise as two women "learning to take charge of their lives...exercising what in the past have been male prerogatives on the screen"?[8] Or, are they simply brazen, lawless adolescents, whose enraged retribution at male abuse is a vicious, self-indulgence — an overreaction to past traumas and present inadequacies?

Do you feel their choices demonstrate "toxic feminism"?[9] Are their acts just the farcical, charming misdirections of lovely, sensual women ("ebullient," as one reviewer termed it) sowing a tediously large quantity of repressed wild oats?

You may think this movie is a comedy, full of quaint, folksy characters and dialogue. Two friends of mine said they enjoyed this movie only after they stopped looking for a deep message. This may be your sense too.

Janet Maslin, writing in *The New York Times* considers the film's ending invigorating:

> ...its heroines, during the course of a few brief but wildly eventful days, crystallize their thoughts and arrive at a philosophical clarity that would have been unavailable to them in their prior lives...they take full charge of their lives and full responsibility for their missteps.[10]

Within the context of what you're told about these friends, do you see their final solution as bold heroism or "philosophical clarity"? As the trapped two smile bravely at each other, hold hands, and choose an explosive death (over what they sense to be certain imprisonment — life in jail or spent in their former, lesser existence), do you interpret this as love?

Or do you wonder if they aren't really sadomasochists? (One reviewer writes, "The movie is astonishing because its heroines are so relentlessly, hopelessly stupid.")[11]

3. *After viewing:* Consider how, or if, the movie adds value to your humanity. What did you learn? What stays with you? Are there lessons or insights here that you'd hope your child would carry away?

As noted earlier, I tried to imagine how anyone (man, woman, or child) might act if they were in the same circumstances as *Thelma & Louise* and yearned to be heroic, virtuous, a fully human or free. I took the film's ending seriously, and didn't like it.

The heroines' Americanized *seppuku* (hara-kiri) left me (as well as the last image: a freeze-frame of the women's blue convertible) up in the air. Were these women tough, would-be independent warriors or confused self-saboteurs? Writing in *Chronicles,* Janet Scott Barlow felt the ending shrunk its heroines, made them:

> ... visually incidental to the effect of an automobile suspended over a canyon.... More than once... the supposedly worldly wise Louise says to the flea-brained Thelma, "You get what you settle for." Ain't it the truth. That should be the slogan of moviegoers weary of films filled with tiny women.[12]

Seppuku is a noble human act, an art of high intention, a fully thought-out choice supporting a tight web of single-minded, heroic acts. The hero's death means to forward some consistent, philosophical idea.[13] For instance, Gary Cooper's solitary confrontation with the outlaws in *High Noon* forces an examination of conscience. Would we — like the townspeople whom Cooper represents as sheriff — back away from violence or bullies? For what do we stand, sacrifice, risk all, if anything? *High Noon,* suggests Ann-

Janine Morey, is "a film about the efficacy of individual and community action, the efficacy of violence and force to uphold peace and non-violence, and ... the positions of women and men in the working out of such questions.... It asks [us] ... what price is necessary for self-respect ... what it is we think we will answer to and for."[14]

The gifted Japanese writer Yukio Mishima (who at forty-five, in 1970, dramatically plunged a sword into his abdomen in public) wrote that the business of the samurai is the business of death.

> Our task is a curious, uncertain one. On the surface it is harsh, but to me it seems a task very like a poem. There is nothing so important to us as purity. Here [at this training camp, we live as if in a scientific laboratory], we are conducting an experiment in purity, with an eye to the uncertain future.[15]

Hara-kiri is laced through and through with sadistic-masochistic overtones. Fanatic love, need for surrender and death, the experience of inner peace as tedious, unendurable boredom, the endless self-punishing disciplines (designed to train mind, body, and will to "choose death when faced with a choice between life and death"), all these, as John Nathan, Mishima's scholarly, empathic biographer writes, are precursors to calling oneself samurai.

Like Mishima, the samurai requires "an alternative to that ... lifelessness of peace." This alternative, typically, is symbolized by the sword. Mishima's private papers romanticize and eroticize death, another sadomasochistic trait.

> We feel no pain. This is the death of bliss. Yet as we move the sword lodged so firmly in our flesh we hear the sobbing behind us of our men who have followed us into battle.... Our generalissimo descends from his

white horse and stands on the snow dyed scarlet with
our young blood. At his feet lie our bodies now about
to die. As we move toward death our majesty salutes
us.[16]

Masochists also project their power. They give away
their potential for magnificence to cruel, dominating individuals. (Mishima wrote, "In all honesty, I am fascinated with Hitler...[he] was a political genius, but not
a hero...I feel one hundred times more sympathetic to
Mussolini...").[17]

Thelma puts her vile spouse in the driver's seat of
her life; Louise — ultimately — looks to Thelma for answers. Did Thelma and Louise drive over the cliff because
of a similar inability to tolerate peace? Did their desire
for death *build* during their stimulating — if simultaneously horrendous — ordeal? Did these two confront their
demons, as do authentic heroes, say, Sheriff Will Kane in
High Noon? Questions like these are unending and stimulate self-study through discussion and personal journal
work.

It certainly isn't necessary to delve into a movie's
subplots and intricacies, *unless* we're disquieted by some
scene — for better or worse, as were many who reacted
turbulently to *Thelma & Louise.* If you did, too, then you
might explore its related psychological or social issues
more thoroughly.

For instance, is this movie about heroism or the maso-
chist's mode of communication that invites trouble? Even
when another individual (particularly controlling types)
are merely unresponsive or expressionless, masochists
imagine the other is angry. They also reject their own fury.

People who eroticize surrender, who find greater thrill
in relinquishment of life than in working patiently through
its dull, tough rigors are often overeager to please. Not

surprisingly, as *Thelma & Louise* reveals, the unwillingness to express what we feel or need breeds rage. Dr. Natalie Shainess, a psychiatrist specializing in such communication disorders, explains the machinations of this phenomenon:

> Continual self-abasement certainly breeds anger and resentment, and while the masochistic person guards vigilantly against any display of these feelings, occasionally they erupt. The docile, yielding accommodator can, every so often, lash out in a hostile fashion. At a glance this may be seen as an improvement over her ordinarily immutable submissiveness. In fact, it is no improvement at all, for her anger is usually expressed inappropriately and ends up causing her just as much trouble as her subservience.[18]

Or *more* trouble than before. Masochists put "giant masks" on people, as poet Robert Bly conceives the process. He outlines the unfolding drama when women project their negative patriarchal powers onto men who won't live up to that role:

> What if [those others] fail to be a negative patriarch? What to do then?...She might, unconsciously of course, overdraw her checking account, lose bills, dent the fender, feel victimized, act like a little girl. That may turn him into a tyrant again. Or she may go to a feminist meeting to be revved up. Hopefully someone there will explain that even men's kindness are a subtle part of their oppression. When she gets home he has the patriarch mask on again.[19]

We can view *Thelma & Louise* variously: They're either desperado-heroines or knee-jerk masochists, or something else. Louise has enormous potential for heroism. She's deep, and thoughtful, and possesses an inherent dignity.

She's wise and responsible. Louise has overcome significant personal pain. Yet she subverts her power, relin-
quishes her life's control to the giddy Thelma.

In one scene, Louise meticulously instructs Thelma
about carefully guarding her money. Louise addresses
Thelma as one might a youngster with questionable judgment. Louise waits until she has Thelma's full attention.
She speaks slowly and carefully. Seemingly Louise knows
who she's dealing with. "You're holding our future in your
hands," she cautions meaningfully, giving Thelma her life's
savings.

Thelma fulfills her friend's worst prophecy. She leaves
Louise's entire bankroll in plain sight, on *top* of a dresser
(they're staying at a cheap motel), *then* invites in a sexy
stranger for a few hours' sensuous frolic in bed. *Then*
Thelma leaves him alone, unattended, in the room, while
she casually strolls over to the motel café to tell Louise,
over a leisurely breakfast, all about her "good sex." (In-
credibly, Thelma does all this *after* hearing her drifter-lover
brag about his prowess as an armed robber.) Even a
ten-year-old child could predict the inevitable disastrous
consequences of such choices. Neither Dirty Harry, B. L.
Stryker, nor the Terminator would ever sink so low.

One reviewer states that without these twists there
would be no story and no excitement. Yet heroic women
have appeared in typically "men's roles" and disproved
this. Geneviève Bujold, Jamie Lee Curtis, Jane Fonda,
Theresa Russell, and Debra Winger respectively in their
various doctor, cop, lawyer, hooker, detective roles, and
even the more fragile, impish Goldie Hawn in her performances (as hooker, poor-rich-girl, or victim) manage to
raise pulses and capture audience attention despite their
obvious shrewdness and charismatic or cerebral power.

Thelma and Louise stubbornly demonstrate the
repetitive-compulsive behaviors of masochists (male or fe-

male; this neurosis has no gender). Watching the two friends unsuccessfully analyze their predicament, noticing that they possess zero negotiation skill, give no thought to the fact that they're fleeing a non-crime (they're told this repeatedly, but choose not to hear), one assumes they lack *desire* to reconcile conflict with words, language, or rational thought. These attributes are all facets of human power, something — for all this supposed "liberation" — they're missing. Seen in this light, *Thelma & Louise* tells us of a wasted life and potential.

The steep price they willingly pay for their "freedom" and female bonding, the exquisitely senseless interlocked, symbiotic nature of their response to each other, is another characteristic of unhealthy coupling.

Dr. Shainess underscores the disturbing irrational dependency of all such pairings:

> The absorbing, all-encompassing...sadomasochistic-masochistic connection [is] illustrated in Ingmar Bergman's film *Wild Strawberries*. A doctor picks up a couple as he is driving along a road. Once in the car, the couple ignores the fact that anyone else is present, continuing the horrendous argument they were in the midst of when the doctor stopped for them. *All social amenities are displaced, all notions of proper social conduct obliterated by the couple's obsessive need to continue to struggle.*[20] [italics mine]

With *Thelma & Louise*, one eventually asks, "Who's projecting what?"

As we examine our varying responses (especially the intense ones), we can construct bridges of understanding between a story and our psyches. Here is where it helps to stay centered. If we're off balance — outraged, anxious, closed-minded, or opinionated — we never will objectively see the images, ideas, or attitudes that sit on the screen of our own mind.

The quieting-down method I outlined in *A Way Without Words* is useful in preparation for reflective movie-viewing. The technique measurably improves alertness, receptivity to new ideas, and normalizes our breath. It paves our way to better absorb the content of any story, is both simple and significant, a distillation of ancient methods I've studied over some thirty years of comparing classical meditation practices. We can easily apply the process to our study of movies — to let us *experience* our visual encounters.

An Experiment in Balance

In preparation for each viewing session, consider your present disposition, posture (i.e., your body's attitude), and the way you're sitting. Let your attention move effortlessly, without strain, first to your body, then to your breath, until consciousness joins breath — becomes breath. Simply inhale and exhale naturally. Don't add anything extra; just pay attention.

Follow your breath in this innocent, watchful way for a few minutes. Notice any tension or holding. Let your breath travel into these spots, as you grow aware of them. To release tension you may experiment with "breathing into" any part of your body that feels strained. Never force your breath.

Your gentle attention is sufficient to spontaneously deepen and correct your breathing if it's constricted. *Experience your condition* without inner criticizing or comment. If you notice yourself judging or narrating, simply *listen* to the tone of your inner dialogue. Objectively "follow judgment" as you follow breath.

If you've brought any worries to your film-viewing session, consciously lay these aside. (You can always get them again later, after the session.) During this quieting-down time, some find (or create) their own private thought-language: pictures, symbols, or cues by which they inform themselves of their own biases or questions.[21]

One man told me he asked his mind to remind him whenever he was holding his breath:

> This works. I watch movies *and* I'm aware as my chest tightens up with tension. Paying attention is all it takes to release the stress. Ironically, I'm getting more out of a film this way. The method has shown me my overreactions. I use it at work and when I'm listening to my kids.

As soon as you're calm and centered, start watching a movie. (If you go to a theater, just recollect yourself unobtrusively before giving your attention to the screen.) If and as you're able, notice your breathing from your inner vantage point — your subtle, always-present witness or intuitive core. After a while, this becomes automatic.

Observe how your inmost energies and breath are affected by the movie's images, ideas, conversations, and characters — especially when these throw you off balance, take you away from your self-possession. In all likelihood, a film's stimulants separating you from your inmost self are similar to whatever unbalances you in daily life.

Laughing also stimulates deep breathing. When we're at ease, breathing is organic; it happens without control or interference. The Buddhist saying, "Life breathes us," explains this experience. Following breath improves comprehensions of what breath says to us. For example, I've met numerous adults who, prior to working with their breathing, think of their anger (and other emotions) in stereotypical, childish ways.

They believe anger always expresses itself in combative or hostile expression or that only sadness gives rise to tears. After sensitizing themselves to the unique patterns of their own breathing, they notice that their anger turns inward, releases itself through apathy, loss of caring, or diminished purposefulness, or in overeating or bizarre sleeping habits.

Anger generates tears (as can joy or grief), and voice or posture shifts. I've heard both men and women say that, as self-awareness deepens, they discover their eyes predictably water from bottled-up rage or overflowing happiness (two watery terms). Tears are just one of our body's signals that its energies need to express.

Instead of internalizing our feelings, we can learn to be active agents of our excitements. Following breath shows us how to use words, voice, body language, and our overall communications skills appropriately. The nuances of movement and expression become messengers to release stress or pent-up emotion.

The more we inhibit our breath, the more unaware we are of our habitual blocks to concentration, and, correspondingly, the greater our overall resistance toward learning and new experiences. The angry kid in the classroom who doesn't *hear* the teacher illustrates the connection between growth, learning, and constricted breathing.

Deep, healthful breathing assists the body's balance and our learning. Recollecting our shared early experience almost all of us know why every good kindergarten teacher insists that five-year-olds rest, or calm down, before changing from one learning activity to another.

Correcting the "Dummy-Reflex"

Some self-collection seems in order prior to, and during, *any* study session or film viewing. We must make proper, full contact with a circumstance or we gain no value from it. Unless we "put our teeth" into the matter — engage ourselves with it, chew it up aggressively, assimilate it — we cannot fully tackle the thing at hand.[22]

A disturbing facet of today's educational system (and our excessively passive movie and TV viewing habits) is that these don't teach us to fully engage with tasks. We use phrases like "veg out" or "zone out" to describe how we handle (or attempt to manage) stress.

We frequently pride ourselves on doing several things at once. We eat, talk on the car phone, *and* drive. We exercise, read the newspaper, *and* watch TV. When friends visit, the TV or stereo — usually housed at center stage of the living room — blares on. Moreover we want something for nothing, expect our food, answers, and monetary or career success instantly.

F. S. Perls contended many adults adopt a "dummy-reflex" — try to get something for nothing, without any real expenditure of effort. The dummy-reflex seriously impedes our "development of personality."[23] We never appreciate the validity of the reality principle: that we must *actively appropriate benefit* from persons or situations in order to gain something of lasting value.

As we watch movies, our mystical messages (or spiritual insights) arrive when we pay attention to the story *and* to ourselves, actively learn to "see," work to understand, chew up whatever we receive. By experiencing ourselves as able, causal agents of our learning, we discover we're fully capable of changing the structure of events. We're effectual discerners — able to distinguish between our projections, fantasies, and discomforts and the actual realities around us.

The alternative — vegging or zoning out, adopting a dummy-reflex — means that we never transform ourselves or elevate our spiritual sights through vital encounter with our direct experience. Following breath seems one uncomplicated curative to our all-too-human tendency to become robotic, wooden, and sleepy (bored) while reading, watching TV or while in the presence of others.

7

This may seem to you melodramatic,
but indulge me, please,
I like melodrama.

—Quintanilla
The Conspirators[1]

EXERCISE YOUR
"SPIRITUAL EYES"

... the spiritual art, the most difficult of the arts ... is an invisible, hidden art which is understood only through purity of heart....

—Saint John Cassian

While I wrote this book, a few editor friends previewed my manuscript with lively interest. They all described their favorite movies, urging me to list my own "top fifty" — the movies I've watched for spiritual or inspirational value. It seems easy enough to enumerate two or three hundred movies that I've enjoyed, but outlandish to limit myself to just fifty. This seems like being asked to exclude a huge and colorful assortment of friends from some personally significant celebration. Nevertheless, I've generated a grouping (minus comedies, musicals, and foreign films), for both *following love* and *following virtue*, adding a few subjective remarks about my preferences.

I've listed only pictures that don't tire me, even after embarrassingly frequent viewings. I make no neat, mechanical separations between "love" and "virtue" as I watch. These two qualities pop out at me; hopefully their corresponding attributes flow together (as do mind

151

and body) into one, seamless essence. For the purposes of discussion and exercise, however, the distinction seems useful.

Love & Virtue: My "Favorites"

Love is so much more than romance, more than personal, "special" affections. Love sparks love. Love motivates. Love reminds us of life's intrinsic worth and stimulates our "yes-response" to people, to adventure, to existence. Love is frequently indirect. It beckons us unexpectedly from any and all surprising, hidden corners. Love has unobtrusively saved my life too many times to mention.

Years ago, I suffered keen, personal loss when a dear friend died. Grieving badly, unable to sleep, one early morning I took a drive along Malibu's Pacific Coast Highway — a long stretch of freeway that for miles parallels the sea. Mine was one of but a few lonely cars in sight. Normally I happily anticipate sunrise drives along the ocean, but not this wretched dawn.

I am only half aware of the water's leaden, cold presence. Sky and sand are dreary gray — like me. Suddenly, at the farthest edge of the horizon, I spot a hot, crimson dot — bold and captivating. Red-Dot speeds toward me, piercing through my misery as it approaches. In the twinkling of an eye, reality shifts.

Sharp, strong color and beauty (in this case, impeccable design — Red-Dot turns out to be a sleek, 940 Porsche, a car I've long desired) punctures my morose preoccupations. Bright, pure tones and master craftsmanship draw me, appreciatively, into the moment, remind me of e.e. cummings's lines, "I who have died am alive again today, and this is the sun's birthday." Immediately I am cheered — even jovial.

When, like racy red sports cars, some nuance in a film restores our joy, cuts through our deadness, or reflects our feeling that we want to be and do more, that's love. Love always stimulates life.

I'm a sucker for Capra, Spielberg, Scorsese, and Hitchcock films. I love old black-and-white pictures, corny relics about angels, heaven, romance, and life-after-death. I *crave* comedy (including hokey slapstick), spy movies, suspenseful courtroom dramas, and mysteries (especially those that take place on trains, ships, and in glamorous hotels). I never watch evil or sadistic movies that manipulate and exploit our basest instincts or that seed our fear and, when it's a video, I fast-forward through the gore. I loathe films with predictable, explicit violence (generally against helpless women), redundant car chases, and victimization of the weak. And, I detest — forgive me — "docudrama."

I'm thankful for all those actors whose depth, intelligence, and humanity shine through their performances, and I'm touched and inspired by their gifted interpretations of a character. Fine actors inject their *own* life into the most banal or lifeless plot.

Who can forget the poetic impact of artists like Jean Arthur, Ingrid Bergman, Humphrey Bogart, Charles Coburn, and Clifton Webb? Marlon Brando, Michael Caine, Robert De Niro, John Gielgud, Alec Guinness, Walter Matthau, Al Pacino, and Laurence Olivier somehow affect me as did Red-Dot. Similarly, actors like the following have consistently been for me clear, bright truth-tellers:

Fred Astaire	Sean Connery	Clint Eastwood
Kevin Bacon	Billy Crystal	Hector Elizondo
Alec Baldwin	Willem Dafoe	Sally Field
Ann Bancroft	Daniel Day-Lewis	Larry Fishburne
Klaus Maria	Danny DeVito	Andy Garcia
Brandauer	Michael Douglas	James Garner
Geneviève Bujold	Richard Dreyfus	Richard Gere
Ellen Burstyn	Robert Duvall	Mel Gibson

Danny Glover	Kevin Kline	Ralph Richardson
Melanie Griffith	Burt Lancaster	Molly Ringwald
Gene Hackman	Angela Lansbury	Theresa Russell
Tom Hanks	Charles Laughton	Winona Ryder
Ed Harris	Robert Loggia	Susan Sarandon
Barbara Hershey	Myrna Loy	Maggie Smith
Dustin Hoffman	John Malkovich	James Stewart
Anthony Hopkins	Joe Mantegna	Meryl Streep
Holly Hunter	Steve Martin	David Suchet
Jeremy Irons	Bette Midler	Emma Thompson
Glenda Jackson	Jack Nicholson	Meg Tilly
James Earl Jones	Nick Nolte	Rip Torn
Tommy Lee Jones	Gregory Peck	Debra Winger
Raul Julia	Rosie Perez	Christopher Walken
Diane Keaton	Joe Pesci	Denzel Washington
Harvey Keitel	Michelle Pfeiffer	Sigourney Weaver
Ben Kingsley	Sidney Poitier	Peter Weller
	William Powell	

And this just *begins* my list. So many other actors are, to me, love-in-action, pure energy. Their consciousness and presence "breathes into our nostrils the breath of life."

Movies that repeatedly speak to me of love:

Lighter

- *An Affair to Remember*
- *Arsenic and Old Lace*
- *Bagdad Cafe*
- *Beauty and the Beast* (1991)
- *The Bells of St. Mary's*
- *Big*
- *The Bishop's Wife*
- *The Butcher's Wife*
- *Defending Your Life*
- *Drop Dead Fred*
- *Enchanted April*
- *Fantasia* (1940)
- *Ferris Bueller's Day Off*
- *The Ghost and Mrs. Muir*
- *Going My Way*
- *Heaven Can Wait* (1978)

Heavier

- *The African Queen*
- *Biloxi Blues*
- *Boyz N the Hood*
- *The Breakfast Club*
- *The Bridge on the River Kwai*
- *Casablanca*
- *Cinema Paradiso*
- *Close Encounters of the Third Kind*
- *Dances with Wolves*
- *Educating Rita*
- *84 Charing Cross Road*
- *Grand Canyon*
- *Hannah and her Sisters*
- *High Noon*
- *Kramer versus Kramer*

Lighter	Heavier
•*Here Comes Mr. Jordan* (1941)	•*Mask*
•*It Happened One Night*	•*Midnight Cowboy*
•*It's a Wonderful Life*	•*Murphy's Romance*
•*Life with Father*	•*Norma Rae*
•*Mr. Belvedere* (series)	•*Notorious*
•*Mr. Smith Goes to Washington*	•*Places in the Heart*
•*Miracle on 34th Street*	•*Rain Man*
•*Moonstruck*	•*Stanley & Iris*
•*Oh, God!*	•*The Thirty-Nine Steps*
•*Parenthood*	•*Tin Men*
•*Roman Holiday*	•*To Kill a Mockingbird*
•*The Secret Life of Walter Mitty*	•*2001: A Space Odyssey*
•*When Harry Met Sally*	•*Whistle down the Wind*

To *follow virtue*, I search out movies about uncommonly gifted, competent, or noble characters. I want to see characters grow in their daring or courage, the skill or nobility of their response, the dignity and depth of their being. The heroes' development is central to me, as is their cerebral cunning and purity of heart.

I *love* movies about creatively intelligent people. For me, virtue flourishes in the Sherlock Holmes' series (those featuring Basil Rathbone and particularly the recent British productions starring Jeremy Brett). Miss Marple, of the Agatha Christie mysteries, is a charmer; I especially adore Joan Hickson's Marple *and* Margaret Rutherford's (although I've heard Agatha Christie didn't much care for Rutherford's portrayal).

Andy Garcia shines with heroic promise in just about all his work; the *Thin Man* movies (with William Powell and Myrna Loy) and Hitchcock classics predictably give us virtuous lead characters. David Suchet, as the "new" Hercule Poirot, has genius. These heroes aren't cloying, pretentious, or self-righteous about their decency. They're just smart, tenacious, impeccable.

Movies that repeatedly speak of virtue:

Lighter	Heavier
• *Adam's Rib*	• *Absence of Malice*
• *Alice*	• *Agnes of God*
• *Amadeus*	• *All About Eve*
• *Auntie Mame*	• *Anatomy of a Murder*
• *Barton Fink*	• *Babette's Feast*
• *Beverly Hills Cop*	• *Birdman of Alcatraz*
• *The Big Easy*	• *Black Widow*
• *Born Yesterday*	• *The Boys from Brazil*
• *Chariots of Fire*	• *Broadcast News*
• *The Devil and Miss Jones*	• *Do the Right Thing*
• *Diner*	• *The French Connection*
• *The Dirty Dozen*	• *Gandhi*
• *Down and Out in Beverly Hills*	• *Gentleman's Agreement*
• *The Enchanted Cottage*	• *The Godfather* (I, II, III)
• *A Fish Called Wanda*	• *Homicide*
• *Flashback*	• *Howard's End*
• *The Freshman*	• *Internal Affairs*
• *The Gods Must Be Crazy*	• *Judgment at Nuremberg*
• *Good Morning, Vietnam*	• *The Maltese Falcon*
• *Goodbye Mr. Chips*	• *Malcolm X*
• *The Great Escape*	• *A Man for All Seasons*
• *The Hero*	• *The Manchurian Candidate*
• *Legal Eagles*	• *Mississippi Burning*
• *Local Hero*	• *An Officer and a Gentleman*
• *Mr. Deeds Goes to Town*	• *One Flew over the Cuckoo's*
• *Other People's Money*	*Nest*
• *Rear Window*	• *Raging Bull*
• *Risky Business*	• *Resurrection*
• *Saving Grace*	• *Serpico*
• *Sherlock Holmes* (series)	• *Stalag 17*
• *The Shoes of the Fisherman*	• *Streets of Gold*
• *Sister Act*	• *Suspicion*
• *The Thin Man* (series)	• *The Ten Commandments*
• *Tootsie*	• *Twelve Angry Men*
• *Wall Street*	• *The Verdict*
• *We're No Angels*	• *Witness for the Prosecution*
• *You Can't Take It with You*	

Mine a Movie's "Gold": Further Reflection

Suggested Viewing:

- *Emma's Shadow*
  Metronome Produktions A/S

- *The Karate Kid*
  Columbia/Delphi II

- *Hobson's Choice*
  British Lion/London

Initially it helps to watch these movies (all three or any one of them) while practicing to follow love, virtue, and breath — the three previously mentioned keys to mining a film's gold. This triune focus is our organizing device. This raises consciousness — opens our spiritual eyes. To recap what was outlined earlier:

First, *follow a movie's love.* Notice whatever exists of compassion or generosity toward self and others. Attend to the film's higher "Being" values — joy, creativity, humor, courage, honesty, etc. These too flow from love.

Next, *follow the virtue.* Be aware of, and trace, any basic decency, purity, or personal power as these develop in a character. In the movies listed above, virtue is easy to spot. Many of these films portray archetypical images of good and bad; they define these in absolute terms. This is, in fact, one way that movies like fairy tales are useful. They clearly depict love, virtue, success, and failure; their stories develop our desire for whatever is good, but without directly preaching.

Throughout, *follow your own breath.* Be sensitive to what's happening to your lungs, chest, or throat. Do nothing more — just stay alert to your own breathing. Normally, when calm and centered, our breathing is steady and uneventful.

To understand your own pattern of emotional comforts or distresses, attend to the subtle changes in your breath as you watch films (or do anything else for that matter). This is, by itself, a classical spiritual discipline, practiced in some fashion by the old desert fathers and Zen masters alike. The point of such interior watchfulness is to develop the virtue of discrimination, the "queen among the virtues," as it was named by Saint John Cassian.

1. Before Viewing

In a notebook and in your own words, jot down some of the ways that movies may have been — or still are — like fairy tales for you. If you're uncertain about this, wait until you've seen *Emma's Shadow*, a Dutch movie complete with subtitles.

This motion picture is a fairy tale containing all the essentials of those simple yet highly instructive stories that have been, throughout history, handed on to children to guide them through life: a testing by and an escape from trouble; help obtained from unusual people, animals, or events; exciting, unpredictable adventures; the chance to develop self-awareness, virtue, and inner resolve.

Consider what role, if any, fairy tales and stories in general (e.g., myths, parables, family legends, etc.) played in your early character formation. For example:

- What were your favorite stories when you were young?

- As a child, were you open or closed to fiction's so-called "irrational," illogical elements?

- Did your family (i.e., those significant adults whom you admired or feared) encourage or belittle your enjoyment of drama, make-believe, or story times?

- What contribution did movies make to the richness of your imagination or fantasy world when you were little?

2. While Viewing

Identify love's energy as it develops in a plot or character and as it deepens your interest in a movie. This task becomes easier *if* you pay attention to your breathing. For instance:

- When do you predictably hold your breath or choke back tears or sigh?

- What scenes, comments, or crisis points seem too much to bear or are overly disturbing? How do you interpret this?

- What does your body seem to be saying to you?

- When "attending to love," can you identify forgiveness, compassion, or mature, selfless love (not necessarily the obvious romantic or lustful affection) as these surface in a character *and* in you?

We see that Emma is a decidedly larger human being, despite her youth, *after* Malthé enters her life with caring, familial involvement. What inner turns do you sense expand Emma's and Malthé's humanity? She seems older at the end of the film, but not because of time having passed.

Similarly, as trust and bonds of affection deepen among various characters in *The Karate Kid* and *Hobson's Choice*, they all change for the better. Following love, we notice everyone (i.e., men, women, children; rich and poor; educated and illiterate) grows kinder, more self-confident and courageous. Love always influences for the better.

Considering love's healing properties, reflect on your own life. Perhaps you are single, newly divorced, widowed, or separated and believe that you can only express love through traditional or formal arrangements: in marriage, through existing community ties or clubs or with friends of your own age and social circle. You may be retired and think you're "too old" to build new relationships. Maybe you're a teenager who feels that romance and passion is all there is to love. In what ways does *Emma's Shadow* enlarge your perspective about love?

3. After Viewing

Think about how others have added value to your humanity. Consider:

- Have you been supporting (placating?) someone who's abusive, who deprives you of love and life, or who dominates, thwarts, or suffocates you?

- How might you correct this gently, productively? (Do you need professional help?)

- How willing are you to think more deeply about these questions, perhaps improving yourself wherever possible in some small, responsible way?

- How open are you to influencing the good in someone else's development, say a friend, neighbor, or a child?

- If not directly, then from a distance, what specific individuals have helped mobilize your virtues or added to your overall well-being?

- Have you ever thought of thanking them?

- In short, what might you do (i.e., what are you willing to do) to "follow the love" in your own life in small, nevertheless significant, ways?

- Watching any or all of these movies, how did your sensibilities on this matter broaden?

- How might your quality of life improve if you found ways to *apply* a more universal, spiritual definition of love to your life's choices?

Awaken Inner Strength: Further Reflection

Suggested Viewing:

- *Babette's Feast*
  Panorama/Nordisk/Danish Film Institute

Virtue asks us to observe what we do and why. At times, it also demands we watch ourselves disintegrate (actually relinquish all that's dear) *without* knowing precisely why.

Virtue clings to abiding, undergirding trust. As we see ourselves go toward the abyss, trust says, "I — the self within myself, the living heart behind my social mask — will be reborn again, at a future point in time if not right here and now." All this means activating our good will and our personal agency so fully, so intentionally, that ultimately we affirm life — mysteriously unify ourselves with all of life.

By cultivating love and inner strength, we grow secure enough to manage this, our primary human assignment. Whatever else we may accept as life tasks, awakening inner strength is first.

Babette's Feast, directed by Gabriel Axel (from author Isak Dinesen's story), is set in a nineteenth-century context as far removed from our affluent Western life as is the North Pole from the South. Yet we can empathize with these characters — both minor and major — because they are exactly like us. We know them as we know ourselves — kindred spirits, part of the human species.

When we meet Babette she is devastated, a refugee who's lost everything: family, financial security, social standing, and home. Her gentleness, her steadfast, unassuming dignity teach us that something vital — some quiet hidden power — still shines in her.

Babette's virtue is obvious and universal. She breathes life into the scriptural injunction that those who would be first make themselves last. She validates the Buddhist wisdom:

> *We live happily indeed, though we call nothing our own!*
> *We shall be like bright gods, feeding on happiness.*[2]

Movie critic Richard Schickel reminds us that true artists need so little to get along: time, solitude, a bit of cash to buy supplies, supportive friends. He partially explains Babette's poise and bearing, suggesting that their source is in her "extraordinary talent." Babette has more — she possesses spiritual maturity:

> ...how rarely artists themselves confront their difficulties in an engaging spirit. The whine of self-pity, the bombast of self-aggrandizement, the low moan of tragedy are the notes most often heard from [creators on the subject of their lives].[3]

As suggested, each of us has an Inner Artist whose energies and intelligence fund our talents, virtues, and spiritual renewal. As with Babette, these can empower our rebirth.

1. Before Viewing

Consider what the word "wholeness" means to you. Try defining it precisely. Or describe it generally in your journal without leaning too heavily on others' words or opinions.

2. While Viewing

Take notes (if you're so inclined) about those scenes, symbols, colors, characters, and conversations or feelings that touch you. Reach into your significant viewing instances to discern the nature of your emotional reactions.

- *What* do these scenes tell you? (Not "why" do you feel as you do, but rather *what* does your subjective life say to you?)

- When — during what scenes — do you hold your breath?

- What does your breath say to you when you hold it?

- How did your breath alert you — tell you what you felt?

Stretch into your responses as you watch. Don't settle for trivial answers. Discover what your private, interior movements, your turnings of spirit seem to communicate.

3. After Viewing

Note your reaction to the story, its characters and conclusion.

- How do all these facets resonate with your values, personal outlook, your goals and life as a whole?

- What, if any, elements of wholeness does Babette embody in your eyes?

- How do some of the other characters affect you: i.e., in what ways do their personal power, virtue, and general conduct touch you — for better or worse?

- What, if any, new appreciations for your life's little earthly delights did you gain from watching this movie? In what ways does pleasure relate to spirituality?

- What place does celebration have in your life? To what extent does your ability to celebrate contribute to your pleasures and emotional healing?

- In the last part of the movie, Babette *asks* to pay for the dinner party out of her own funds. To what extent do you identify with her need to give of herself or use her talents (art; perhaps *things*) to transform life?

- How do you explain the increase of gaiety, warmth, affection, and general extrovertedness of the guests at the feast?

A sample, ongoing commentary from one individual's journal could encourage you to write about your own responses:

- I'm overwhelmed by the degree to which the lack of gaiety, beauty, and celebration robs us of life.

- Without some form of human, earthly love we die. Little wonder that the town's elders in this movie are so full of rancor and melancholia. Without joy, even our talents drain away. I am thankful that the two sisters had each other....

- My appreciation for my own simple, tangible delights is renewed: my rose garden, those old blue and white dishes that I found at auction, my good health, and friends with whom to savor all these "things."

- The particulars of life seem highly charged with meaning now. I'm hooked into some overriding purpose. I've not experienced this for some time — not since my youth. It's not *things*, but the love behind them that counts for so much ... (no wonder the Lord pronounced "all that He had made as very good").

- I cry when the two angelic-faced but parched sisters show Babette how to cut up that dried flatfish. Those dead, dry cods show what happens to life when we forget to express our joy. Joy is *un*like pleasure: It bubbles up inside me all the time, if I pay attention. . . .

• I breathe easier as Babette finds the means to add small, inexpensive delicacies, like yellow onions, to the family's daily meals. This scene brings the first ray of hope that life will forge its way through grim, false piety — eventually.

Movies like *Babette's Feast, The Godfather* series, *Malcolm X, A Man for All Seasons* deserve our reflection, journal notes, and advanced study or discussion (for instance, in college courses) during which we devote ample time to significant dialogue, mythical scenes, and archetypal symbols. Not *every* film needs — or deserves — such scrutiny.

Probably most movies can be spiritually rewarding even if we merely ask ourselves a few general questions *while* watching. The next two exercises illustrate this point: We can gain spiritual insight even when viewing "superficially" — when relaxing, when we're with friends, without much effort.

Note that the next two viewing exercises omit the structured questions, as with the "before–during–after" journal or discussion process.

In all likelihood, most people will continue to watch their favorite movies while relaxing with family or friends. Perhaps journal-keeping or formal conversation is inappropriate in these settings.

There's no reason to be rigid or doctrinaire about all this. It *is* possible to be self-monitoring without ceremony. Viewing questions for the following films are listed informally — after general overview. One could entertain these in any number of ways, either before, during or after watching the movies.

Follow Virtue: Further Reflection

Suggested Viewing:

- *Grand Canyon*
  Twentieth Century Fox

- *Being There*
  Lorimar/North Star/CIP

- *Lilies of the Field*
  UA/Rainbow

Compare and contrast each main character's embodiment of virtue: generosity, inner peace (no-strife), or courage. How do the movies' main characters portray virtue, as you understand the word?

Consider the questions I offer, capturing whatever insights or emotional information that surfaces as you watch. Remember to notice your breathing (even if you aren't keeping notes). It is most productive to view these movies as soon as possible *after* reading the related chapter.

If you decide to keep your journal available while you're watching, you can record strong or sudden responses during *specific* scenes. Over time, the pattern of these scenes — and your own favorite way of watching movies — can richly inform you of what really matters to *you*.

The beauty of renting a videotape is that you can replay memorable scenes, thereby studying not only the scene but also your impressions of it.

If you discuss these themes with a group of like-minded friends, it is often best if everyone reads the relevant chapter material right before viewing the film (e.g., the same day, night, or week of your meeting, as is done in Book

Clubs) so that follow-up discussions can focus on virtue per se and not ramble on.

It is no more necessary to share your most personal, emotional reactions to a movie than it is to tell everyone your intimate dreams. In all cases, let your own instincts and mature good judgment be your censor and guide. (If you notice a tendency to "tell all," to set yourself up for the unwanted advice of others, or to exploit your private life for use as social small talk, this too is an occasion for further study and self-correction!)[4, 5]

Possible Questions for Journal or Discussion

Grand Canyon:

The opening scenes introduce several characters who are trying to control their fear. Reflecting on your own anxieties (the way you typically avoid risks or stave off dread), is there anything you learned from these heroes and heroines? If not, how would you have changed their reactions to their contemporary experiences? (e.g., having car trouble in a strange downtown neighborhood in any major urban area; living amongst warring gang members, etc.)

How do you explain the fast friendship between the two heroes (Glover and Klein)? Have you ever been immediately drawn to someone from another culture? What happened? Could you let yourself "go with" your feelings of instant rapport? Did you talk yourself out of that relationship?

What's your explanation of the film's ending? How do you interpret the final scene and what does it say about possible ways to reconcile the fears, distrusts, and apprehensions of your own life?

Being There:

Keep in mind that this is a comedy and meant to depict life's truths in a stylized (perhaps artificial) manner. How fully do you relate to, or enjoy, Sellers' character? If you don't, why not? Does his state of mind seem desirable to you?

One person said, "In some ways, Sellers' role illustrates an innocence and simplicity that I admire. Then again, he's so dispassionate that all normal human responses are missing: He has no sexual drive, no self-interested instincts." To this individual, Sellers' character was a turn-off. In what ways is this "no-strife" as you interpret it?

Lilies of the Field:

At some point, the hero, Homer Smith, becomes unthreatened by the loss of wages and moves beyond his own self-interests when building the chapel for the nuns. As you view this movie, what do you think sways him to return to the nuns' compound after he initially leaves?

On occasion, have you abandoned your own plans or goals to care for others in a similar generous way?

Drawing on your life's experience, have you helped others to such an extent that increased love, generosity, gratefulness (i.e., for just being alive), or deep job satisfaction resulted? In what ways was your experience growthful for you? To what extent would you hope for such experiences again? How did these events cultivate your finest impulses or let you reach a point, like Smith, where you surrendered to your best qualities?

- Reflecting further on the virtue called "no-strife," and considering the social issues each film depicts, what *usual* social stresses cause you to get overexcited, stressed, or perhaps burned-out, thus separating you from inner peace?

- As you review your own inclinations, how might a development of added virtue bolster your ability to master your inner disturbances?

- Considering virtue in general, what virtues seem natural to you?

- Which virtues seem just beyond your reach?

- How might you *use* selected movies to open your inner eyes to your own fundamental decencies (or to learn how to encourage these in others — for instance, a young child)?

Follow Love: Further Reflection

Suggested Viewing:

- *Defending Your Life*
  Warner

- *To Kill a Mockingbird*
  U-I

Both contemporary and old classic films can be master teachers about love. Viewing these two dissimilar movies together (or approximately at the same time) allows us to "follow the love."

In particular, these stories may shine a spotlight on our own early life when love was (or was not) available to us in nurturing, life-supporting doses, or help us recall how fear (or other negatives) intrudes on our ability to love. We need not keep a journal to grow. Simply letting a movie's honest themes and lessons wash over us seems sufficient to reawaken our particular truths.

In *To Kill a Mockingbird,* Gregory Peck's portrayal of small-town lawyer Atticus Finch is, among other things, a story of the "good father." Finch is steady, firm, and empathic. He's warmly loving. His character could spur glad or sorrowful memories as we consider our own childhood, reminding us of what we did and did not receive from our parents.

Similarly, although a wholly different type of movie, *Defending Your Life* explores how fear thwarts life, limits our very capacity to love or to take risks on behalf of what we know to be our good.

How do these movies restore your memories of your own diverse, loving sensibilities? Alone, or with friends, review your childhood with its unique coloration of traumas and charm. How did you learn to run from, or relate to and love, others?

Create your own mental-movie about the high points of your parents' example and their expectations of you: How did these shape your current ability to press through difficulty, or move beyond fear, or love others?

Both of these movies (and countless others with a similarly evolved degree of complexity) seem rich enough to stimulate memory of what was or to generate mythic images about how life could be better — what it might be, at its best.

Considering movies in this self-reflective way, we learn to see. Over time and with practice we could even develop discernment. (I suspect this depends on the skill of the person who's watching.)

The Growth of Discernment

Good movies are, paradoxically, at once both gentle and forceful. Just like books, their stories can absorb us fully yet let us be. Motion pictures engage our "active-passivity" — that doing/nondoing function of mind required for all creative thinking (and especially for invention's incubation phase).[6, 7]

Movies are amazingly polite, nonintrusive hosts. They never make us speak (as we watch, we needn't move our vocal chords one iota), and they let us daydream amiably. Walker Percy describes this precise phenomenon (from a decidedly different vantage point) in his superb novel *The Moviegoer:*

> Now and then my friends stop by, all gotten up as young eccentrics with their beards and bicycles, and down they go to the Quarter to hear some music and find some whores and still I wish them well. As for me, I stay home...and turn on TV. Not that I like TV so much, but it doesn't distract me from the wonder. That is why I can't go to the trouble they go to. It is distracting, and not for five minutes will I be distracted from the wonder.[8]

Amen. Film stimulates our nonconscious realms delightfully. It offers the mind a chance to recreate (and what a relief this is, considering the frantic world we're in). Thus does mind spin 'round freely in its infinite orbs. As it goes, it seizes this or that surprise or unexpected treasure from its hidden reserves. If we remain alert to these happenings, remain alert and conscious of mind's playful turnings, discernment grows.

We bring our insights and observations from this sort of conscious film-viewing into everyday life. Certainly this seems one reasonable goal. The steps suggested throughout these chapters are but easy, mindful techniques that add to objective self-awareness.

The Zen saying, "what you do, do that," applies as

much to film-viewing as it does to anything else, say chopping wood and carrying water. Moreover, the stories of our lives — our losses and gains, our vices and virtues — seem universal. We remember who we are — as members of an enduring human family — by being open to other people's stories. Such openness also stirs discernment, being as it is akin to honesty. Eventually discernment turns to wisdom.

Saint John Cassian (mentioned earlier) wrote frequently about human virtue. To him, and other early desert fathers, discernment was "the most difficult" of all spiritual arts.

Its cultivation required persistent discipline. It still does. In all these centuries nothing much has changed. Why should we not use film, selectively, as yet one more way to grow strong in this art of arts, to help ourselves become truthful and empathic — toward ourselves and others?

Refined objective awareness — that rare blend of judgment, rational prowess, heightened perception, the integration of intuition and logic — is a benchmark of our spiritual maturity. We don't gain discrimination power from books or experts or college degrees. Life itself is our teacher.

Everything placed in our path can help us assimilate, and learn from, direct experience so that, ultimately, wisdom results. Certain films — like certain lovely people, glorious works of art or music, and special instances of prayer — seem a grace expressly given for our edification. Movies are now our shared, celluloid tradition of storytelling and encouragement.

As we stay fully conscious while eating hamburgers or listening to our child complain of school bullies or viewing movies; as we apply ourselves faithfully to *whatever* we do, discernment blossoms. Following love, virtue, and our own breath, we enter the sacred, luminous present. This in itself is the gift — real power, life itself.

Notes

Introduction

1. W. E. Vine, *Expository Dictionary of New Testament Words* (Nashville: Thomas Nelson, 1952), p. 537.

2. Martin Buber, *The Way of Response* (New York; Schocken Books, 1966), p. 136.

3. While editing the final draft of this manuscript, I read Charlotte Joko Beck's fine book *Everyday Zen* (San Francisco: HarperCollins, 1989), in which she too uses the phrase, *following the breath*. The term is not original with me. Beck, an accomplished Zen teacher, also suggests other words: "It doesn't matter what our practice is called: following the breath, shikantaza, koan study; basically we're all working on the same issues: 'Who are we? What is our life? Where did we come from? Where do we go?' It's essential to living a whole human life that we have some insight." (p. 9).

4. Marsha Sinetar, *A Way Without Words* (Mahwah, NJ: Paulist Press, 1992).

5. Gualala Video (707-884-1050) carries, on standard VCR, almost all the films I mention in this book. (I should add that I've not discussed movies released after early Spring, 1992.)

6. Ananda K. Coomaraswamy, *The Transformation of Nature in Art* (New York: Dover Publications, 1934).

7. Abraham Maslow, *Toward a Psychology of Being* (New York: D. Van Nostrand Co., 1962), p. 58.

1: Reel Power

1. Ephesians 1:18
2. Fritz Perls, *Ego, Hunger and Aggression* (New York: Vintage Books, 1969), p. 157.
3. Meher Baba, *Path of Love* (New York: Samuel Weiser, 1976), p. 99.
4. Robert Lauder, "It's a Wonderful Life: Divine Benevolence" in *Image & Likeness,* ed. John R. May (Mahwah, NJ: Paulist Press, 1990), p. 136.
5. Ananda Coomaraswamy, *The Transformation of Nature in Art* (New York: Dover Publications, 1934).
6. Ananda Coomaraswamy, *What Is Civilisation?* (Great Barrington, ME: Lindisfarne Press, 1989), p. 10.
7. Marsha Sinetar, *Living Happily Ever After* (New York: Villard Books, 1990).
8. Ibid.
9. Video rights to *Emma's Shadow* are controlled by Fox Lorber Associates, 419 Park Ave. South, New York, NY 10016.

2: Adopt New Stories and States of Mind

1. Jean Renoir in *Film Makers on Film Making,* vol. 2, ed. by Joseph McBride, American Film Institute (Los Angeles: J. P. Tarcher, Inc., 1983), p. 44.
2. W. J. Weatherby, *Chariots of Fire* (New York: Dell/Quicksilver Books, 1981), p. 139.
3. Ibid., p. 142.
4. Roger Ebert, *Roger Ebert's Movie Home Companion* (New York and Kansas City: Andrews & McMeel, 1990 ed.), p. 450.
5. Bruno Bettelheim, *The Uses of Enchantment* (New York: Vantage Books ed., 1977), p. 142.
6. Ibid.
7. J. Marion, M. Holmberg, "Home Alone" *TV Guide* vol. 39, August 17–23, 1991, no. 33, #2003, p. 7.
8. Carolyn G. Heilbrun, *Writing Woman's Life* (New York: Ballantine Books, 1958), p. 37.

9. Marsha Sinetar, *Developing a 21st-Century Mind* (New York: Villard Books, 1991).

10. John Briggs, *Fire in the Crucible* (Los Angeles: Jeremy P. Tarcher, 1990), p. 168.

11. Ibid.

12. Vera John-Steiner, *Notebooks of the Mind* (New York: Harper & Row, 1987), p. 185.

13. I came upon the notion of personal revelations and life-impulses rattling around "in our skulls" in some ancient text, but can't remember where. The phrase speaks to me, and so I've used it.

14. Nikos Kazantzakis in *The Choice Is Always Ours*, ed. by D. Phillips, E. Howes, L. Nixon (Wheaton, IL: Re-Quest Books 1977), p. 32.

15. Ibid.

3: Awaken Inner Strength

1. Marcia Landy, editor, *Imitations of Life* (Detroit: Wayne State University Press, 1991), p. 14.

2. *Halliwell's Film Guide*, 7th ed. (New York: Harper & Row, 1989), p. 234.

3. Natalie Shainess, *Sweet Suffering* (New York: Wallaby Books/Pocket Books, 1984).

4. Pam Cook, "Melodrama and the Women's Picture" in *Imitations of Life*, ed. by Marcia Landy, p. 254.

5. Joseph Campbell, ed., *The Portable Jung* (New York: Penguin Books, 1971 ed.), p. 12.

6. Bruno Bettelheim, *The Uses of Enchantment* (New York: Vintage Books, 1973), p. 48.

7. *Halliwell's Film Guide*, p. 527.

8. Marsha Sinetar, *A Way Without Words* (Mahwah, NJ: Paulist Press, 1992). Chapter 4 discusses this in detail.

9. D. Phillips, E. Howes, L. Nixon, ed., *The Choice Is Always Ours* (Wheaton, IL: Re-Quest Books, 1977), p. 166.

10. D. T. Suzuki, *The Training of the Zen Buddhist Monks* (New York: Globe Press Books, 1934).

11. John R. May, "The Godfather Films" in *Image & Likeness* (Mahwah, NJ: Paulist Press, 1992).

4: Follow Virtue

1. *Halliwell's Film Guide*, 7th ed. (New York: Harper & Row, 1989), p. 640.
2. Christian D. Larson, *Just Be Glad* (New York: Thomas Y. Crowell Co., 1912), p. 64.
3. Tom O'Brien, *The Screening of America* (New York: Continuum, 1990), p. 179.
4. Jonathan A. Jacobs, *Virtue and Self-Knowledge* (Englewood Cliffs, NJ: Prentice Hall, 1989), pp. 3, 4.
5. Shunryu Suzuki, *Zen Mind, Beginner's Mind* (New York, Tokyo: Weatherhill, 1975). I have added italics.
6. Martin Buber, *Ecstatic Confessions* (San Francisco: Harper & Row, 1985), p. 3.
7. C. J. A. Lee, T. Hand, *A Taste of Water* (Mahwah, NJ: Paulist Press, 1981), p. 19.
8. *Halliwell's Film Guide*, p. 448.
9. Ibid.
10. Brother Lawrence, *The Practice of the Presence of God* (Old Tappan, NJ: Spire Books/Fleming H. Revell, 1980 ed.).
11. J. G. Bennett, *Is There "Life" on Earth?* (New York: Stonehill, 1973).
12. Marsha Sinetar, *Elegant Choices, Healing Choices* (Mahwah, NJ: Paulist Press, 1988).
13. Peter Browning, ed., *John Muir: In His Own Words* (Lafayette, CA.: Great West Books, 1988), p. 25.

5: Follow Love

1. Abraham Maslow, *Toward a Psychology of Being* (New Jersey: D. Van Nostrand Co., 1962), pp. 23–24.
2. *Halliwell's Film Guide*, 7th ed. (New York: Harper & Row, 1989), p. 562.

3. Tom O'Brien, *The Screening of America* (New York: Continuum, 1990), p. 69.

4. Erich Fromm, *Escape From Freedom* (New York: Avon, 1969 ed.), p. 155.

5. Zweig & Abrams, ed., *Meeting the Shadow* (Los Angeles: Jeremy P. Tarcher, 1991).

6. Carl Rogers, *On Becoming a Person* (New York: Houghton Mifflin, 1961), p. 164.

7. Alice Miller, *Drama of the Gifted Child* (New York: Basic Books, 1981), p. 164.

8. Marsha Sinetar, *Living Happily Ever After* (New York: Villard Books, 1990).

9. Thomas Szasz, *The Second Sin* (New York: Anchor Books, 1974).

10. Paul Tillich, *Courage To Be* (New York: Yale University Press, 1952).

11. Judith Williamson, "Man For Our Season," *New Statesman*, vol. 116, no. 2980, May 6, 1988.

12. *Halliwell's Film Guide*, p. 182.

13. Abraham Maslow, *Toward a Psychology of Being* (New York: D. Van Nostrand Co., 1962), p. 45.

14. John Elof Boodin, in *The Choice Is Always Ours*, D. Phillips, E. Howes, L. Nixon, ed. (Wheaton, IL: Re-Quest Books, 1977), p. 135.

15. Saint Augustine, *The Confessions* (New York: Collier Books, 1961), p. 104.

16. Thomas Cleary, *Zen Essence* (Boston: Shambhala, 1989), p. 66.

17. Marsha Sinetar, *Ordinary People as Monks and Mystics* (Mahwah, NJ: Paulist Press, 1986).

18. Robert Bolt, *A Man for All Seasons* (New York: Scholastic Book Services, 1968 ed.).

19. Ibid.

20. W. E. Vine, *Expository Dictionary of New Testament Words* (Nashville: Thomas Nelson, 1952).

6: Follow Breath

1. Genesis 2:7.
2. Fritz Perls, *Ego, Hunger and Aggression* (New York: Vintage Books, 1969), p. 179. Italics in original.
3. Ibid.
4. Marsha Sinetar, *Developing a 21st-Century Mind* (New York: Villard Books, 1991).
5. Diane Cappadona, "Art of Seeing" in *Image & Likeness,* John R. May, ed. (Mahwah, NJ: Paulist Press, 1992), p. 104.
6. Ibid.
7. Claudio Naranjo and Robert E. Ornstein, *On the Psychology of Meditation* (New York: Penguin, 1971), p. 81.
8. Janet Maslin, *Film View: "Thelma and Louise,"* Sunday edition, *The New York Times,* Sec. 2, p. 11, Col. 1, June 16, 1991.
9. Ibid.
10. Ibid.
11. Janet Scott Barlow, "The Incredible Shrinking Woman," *Chronicles,* March, 1992, pp. 18–20.
12. Ibid.
13. William Scott Wilson, trans., *Hagakure: Book of the Samurai* (New York: Avon Books, 1979).
14. Ann-Janine Morey, *"High Noon;* On the Uncertainty of Certainty" in *Image & Likeness,* John R. May, ed.
15. John Nathan, *Mishima* (Boston/Toronto: Little, Brown, 1974), p. 226.
16. Ibid., p. 212.
17. Ibid., p. 252.
18. Natalie Shainess, *Sweet Suffering* (New York: Wallaby Books/Pocket Books, 1984), p. 64.
19. Robert Bly, *Little Book of the Human Shadow* (New York: Harper & Row, 1988), p. 32.
20. Natalie Shainess, *Sweet Suffering,* p. 103.
21. Marsha Sinetar, *Developing a 21st-Century Mind.*
22. Fritz Perls, *Ego, Hunger and Aggression,* p. 179.
23. Ibid.

7: Exercise Your "Spiritual Eyes"

1. *Halliwell's Film Guide*, 7th ed. (New York: Harper & Row, 1989), p. 219.

2. D. Howes, E. Phillips, L. Nixon, ed., *The Choice Is Always Ours* (Wheaton, IL: Re-Quest Books, 1977), p. 400.

3. Richard Schickel, "Dining Well Is the Best Revenge," *Time*, vol. 131, no. 10, March 7, 1988.

4. Marsha Sinetar, *Elegant Choices, Healing Choices* (Mahwah, NJ: Paulist Press, 1988).

5. Natalie Shainess, *Sweet Suffering* (New York: Wallaby Books/Pocket Books, 1984).

6. Vera John-Steiner, *Notebooks of Mind* (New York: Harper & Row, 1987).

7. Marsha Sinetar, *Developing a 21st-Century Mind* (New York: Villard Books, 1991).

8. Walker Percy, *The Moviegoer* (New York: Ivy Books, 1990 ed.), p. 35.

About the Author

From her remote forest home along the Northwest coast, Marsha Sinetar manages to strongly influence contemporary thought about optimal adult functioning. A bestselling, internationally recognized author, educator, and corporate psychologist, Sinetar heads her own human resource advisory firm (Santa Rosa, CA) and currently serves as *Visiting Professor, Leadership Studies* at Gonzaga University in Spokane, WA.

One of the foremost exponents of the practical value of self-actualization, Marsha Sinetar is a sought-after lecturer whose books are increasingly used worldwide in a wide variety of professional settings (universities, therapy groups, and spiritual direction programs). Her published books include the acclaimed *Do What You Love, The Money Will Follow;* the grassroots bestseller, *Ordinary People As Monks and Mystics; Developing a 21st-Century Mind;* and, more recently, *A Way Without Words.*

Of *Reel Power,* Sinetar's latest contribution to the arena of wholesome spiritual growth, the prolific author says, "Film, like poetry, is one of our heart's most subtle agents.... By helping those we mentor (and ourselves) *manage attention,* we further spiritual growth."